Real-Life Math

Tables, Charts, and Graphs

by
Tom Campbell

illustrated by Lois Leonard Stock

J. WESTON
WALCH
PUBLISHER

Portland, Maine

Dedication

To my parents, who taught me
to value education and much more

User's Guide
to
Walch Reproducible Books

As part of our general effort to provide educational materials which are as practical and economical as possible, we have designated this publication a "reproducible book." The designation means that purchase of the book includes purchase of the right to limited reproduction of all pages on which this symbol appears:

Here is the basic Walch policy: We grant to individual purchasers of this book the right to make sufficient copies of reproducible pages for use by all students of a single teacher. This permission is limited to a single teacher, and does not apply to entire schools or school systems, so institutions purchasing the book should pass the permission on to a single teacher. Copying of the book or its parts for resale is prohibited.

Any questions regarding this policy or requests to purchase further reproduction rights should be addressed to:

Permissions Editor
J. Weston Walch, Publisher
321 Valley Street • P. O. Box 658
Portland, Maine 04104-0658

1   2   3   4   5   6   7   8   9   10

ISBN 0-8251-3814-0

Copyright © 1998
J. Weston Walch, Publisher
P. O. Box 658 • Portland, Maine 04104-0658

Printed in the United States of America

Contents

Charts

Reading Charts

Making Charts

How to Use This Series

The Real-Life Math Series is a collection of activities designed to put the math that students are learning into the context of real-world settings. This series contains math appropriate for prealgebra students all the way up to precalculus students. Problems can be used as reminders of old skills in new contexts, as an opportunity to show how a particular skill is used, or as an enrichment activity for stronger students. Because this is a collection of reproducibles, you may make as many copies of each activity as you wish.

Please be aware that this collection does not and should not replace teacher supervision. Formulas are given only in the teaching notes so that students may be asked to figure them out or the teacher may instruct them on the subjects to be covered. Extension suggestions are also included in the teaching notes. Many of these suggestions involve the use of outside experts. If it is not possible to get these presenters to come to your classroom, individual students may make contact with them by phone or visit their office.

We have found a significant number of "real-world" settings for this collection, but it is not a complete list. Let your imagination go, and use your own experience or the experience of your students to create similar opportunities for contextual study.

Foreword

A college professor of mine once explained to our class that there were three kinds of lies, "lies, —— lies, and statistics." His premise for the morning's lecture was that since most Americans had little or no education in reading statistics critically, we were all susceptible to being hoodwinked by number manipulators. This was a course for math majors, and we all wondered when he would get off his soapbox. Unfortunately, he was able to prove his point. Because students rarely read tables and graphs in the context of learning about them, they tend to see any graphically presented, organized piece of information as being necessarily true.

Years later, I watched an engineering supervisor present his error statistics for the first quarter of the year. In his business, two or three errors a quarter was too many, and his department had made five. However, he showed a bar graph of the number of errors in the previous five quarters, with the y-axis going up to 200. The bars in the graph were razor-thin blips at the bottom of the page, so five errors appeared essentially the same as one. As the supervisor received an ovation for his "fine work," I knew that reading charts, graphs, and tables critically needed to be a focus in my classroom. The activities in this book are designed to teach students to use these devices to read and interpret organized data, to organize their own data, and to think about how presentations can affect the way data are interpreted.

— T.E.C.
Portland, ME 1998

1. Quilting

Goal

To read a table and determine information about the materials, sizes, and required cuts for quilts included in the table.

NCTM Standards Addressed

Standard 1: Mathematics as Problem Solving

Standard 2: Mathematics as Communication

Standard 4: Mathematical Connections

Standard 5: Algebra

Standard 6: Functions

Standard 10: Statistics

Teaching Notes

The first table for making a quilt lists how much material is needed. The first column is the size of the quilt, and the next column is the number of 12" × 12" blocks that must be pieced together to make a quilt that size. The rest of the columns list the material needed for each size quilt. The second table lists the cutting requirements for the strips. You may want to point out the subcolumns for colors 1A, 1B, 2A, 2B, and the background, for the various sizes.

Context

Making quilts is a very mathematical undertaking. Not only are the designs geometric, but the process of buying and cutting the material is exacting and demands reading tables carefully. Most quilt patterns include tables like the ones you see here to assist the quilter in making selections and cutting.

Extension Activities

Students could be asked to verify that there is enough of each kind of material in the first table to make the strips in the second table. They could determine whether it would be possible to buy less material in some cases and still have enough (with a little margin for error).

Answers

1. The queen-size quilt should be 90" × 114".

2. Tom needs 832 feet of thread.

3. Tom will need $1\frac{3}{8}$ yards of material for the border of a king-size quilt.

4. Tom will need $2\frac{3}{8}$ yards of that material.

5. He should cut eight 2-inch strips and fourteen 3-inch strips.

6. He should have only $49\frac{1}{2}" - 45\frac{1}{2}" = 4"$ of waste.

7. The material should cost him $19.61.

8. Tom saved $3.94 by buying the material on sale.

1. Quilting

Tom is learning to quilt. On the first day of class, the teacher hands him two tables. They contain information about the material he will need to make this particular pattern, and how he should cut the material. She tells Tom that he needs to choose five or six different materials, two pairs of which must be in the same color family (i.e., both red or both green). The amount of material he must buy and the number of strips of each size that he must cut are based on the size of the quilt he wants to make. All fabric is considered to be 45 inches wide, making the strips a uniform 45 inches long after cutting across the material. Help Tom figure out the answers to the following questions from the tables below.

Required Material Yardages							
Size	No. blocks	Color 1A	Color 1B	Color 2A	Color 2B	Background	Border
54" × 66" (Crib)	20 (4 × 5)	$7/8$ yds	$7/8$ yds	$7/8$ yds	$7/8$ yds	$7/8$ yds	$5/8$ yds
66" × 102" (Twin)	40 (5 × 8)	$1 3/8$ yds	$1 3/8$ yds	$1 3/8$ yds	$1 3/8$ yds	$1 3/8$ yds	1 yd
88" × 114" (Queen)	63 (7 × 9)	$1 3/4$ yds	$1 3/4$ yds	$1 3/4$ yds	$1 3/4$ yds	$1 7/8$ yds	$1 1/8$ yds
114" × 114" (King)	81 (9 × 9)	$2 1/2$ yds	$2 1/2$ yds	$2 1/2$ yds	$2 3/4$ yds	$2 5/8$ yds	$1 3/8$ yds

Strip Cutting Requirements											
Size	Color 1A		Color 1B		Color 2A		Color 2B	Background			Border
	2"	3"	2"	3"	2"	3"	3"	2"	3"	4"	$3 1/2$"
Crib	3	5	3	5	3	5	7	2	5	1	7
Twin	6	10	6	10	6	10	14	4	10	2	10
Queen	8	14	8	14	8	14	19	5	14	3	11
King	11	21	11	21	11	21	30	7	18	5	13

(continued)

1. **Quilting** (continued)

1. The blocks of this quilt are 12 inches square. The blocks are sewn together. Then a 3-inch wide border is sewn around the outside. One of the dimensions given in the "size" column of the first table has a typo. Which dimension is it?

    _____

2. Tom needs thread to sew the quilt. It will take 18 feet of thread for each block plus four times the length of the perimeter of the finished quilt. How much thread should Tom buy for a twin quilt?

    _____

3. If Tom decides to make a king-size quilt, how much material will he need for the border?

    _____

4. If Tom decides to make a twin-size quilt and use his choice for color 1B as his border material as well, how much of that material should he buy?

    _____

5. Tom has decided on a queen-size quilt. He has washed and ironed his material, in case of shrinking. How many 2-inch strips and how many 3-inch strips should he cut of color 2A?

    _____

6. Assuming that Tom cuts the proper number of strips in question 3, how much waste will he have from what he purchased?

    _____

7. Material is on sale for $2.49 a yard. How much will the material for a twin-size quilt cost?

    _____

8. Material normally costs $2.99 a yard. How much did Tom save by getting it on sale?

    _____

2. Hat Sizes

Goal

To read a chart and determine hat sizes and head measurements based on the information in the chart.

NCTM Standards Addressed

Standard 2: Mathematics as Communication

Standard 4: Mathematical Connections

Standard 5: Algebra

Standard 6: Functions

Standard 10: Statistics

Teaching Notes

We look at tables and charts every day to gather information. Hat sizes seem mysterious because they have little obvious connection to the measurements of the head. In fact, the size is determined by a ratio of the circumference of the head in inches divided by 3.14 (π).

Context

Most clothing measurements, such as for pants, mention inseam length and waist circumference, and are understandable. Other sizing is less obvious. Most of us wear hats; many of them are adjustable, but some are fitted. The chart on page 5 is used by haberdashers in determining hat size. It is the kind of table/chart students might use in ordering from a catalog.

Extension Activities

- Ask students to measure each others' or family members' heads and determine their hat size.

- Ask students to try to discover the formula used to determine size (mentioned in Teaching Notes).

Answers

1. The Mad Hatter should make a size $7\frac{1}{2}$ hat.

2. Kirsi's hat size is $7\frac{5}{8}$.

3. Amanda's hat size is $7\frac{1}{8}$.

4. Jel's head measures $26\frac{5}{8}$ inchs.

5. Riel's head measures 59.5 cm.

6. The next line of the chart should read "Size $8\frac{5}{8}$; 27 inches; 69.5 centimeters."

Name _____   Date _____

2. Hat Sizes

Many hats are adjustable, but some are still sized. These include cowboy hats, top hats, dress hats, bonnets, and fitted baseball caps. Most hat stores use a chart like the one below to find a person's hat size by measuring the circumference of their head. Using the chart, identify the correct size or measurement in the questions on the following page.

Hat Size	Circumference in Inches	Circumference in Centimeters	Hat Size	Circumference in Inches	Circumference in Centimeters
$6\frac{3}{4}$	$21\frac{1}{4}$"	54.5 cm	$7\frac{3}{4}$	$24\frac{3}{8}$"	62.5 cm
$6\frac{7}{8}$	$21\frac{5}{8}$"	55.5 cm	$7\frac{7}{8}$	$24\frac{3}{4}$"	63.5 cm
7	22"	56.5 cm	8	$25\frac{1}{8}$"	64.5 cm
$7\frac{1}{8}$	$22\frac{3}{8}$"	57.5 cm	$8\frac{1}{8}$	$25\frac{1}{2}$"	65.5 cm
$7\frac{1}{4}$	$22\frac{3}{4}$"	58.5 cm	$8\frac{1}{4}$	$25\frac{7}{8}$"	66.5 cm
$7\frac{3}{8}$	$23\frac{1}{8}$"	59.5 cm	$8\frac{3}{8}$	$26\frac{1}{4}$"	67.5 cm
$7\frac{1}{2}$	$23\frac{1}{2}$"	60.5 cm	$8\frac{1}{2}$	$26\frac{5}{8}$"	68.5 cm
$7\frac{5}{8}$	24"	61.5 cm			

1. The Mad Hatter, a haberdasher in Portland, Maine, takes a phone order for a hat. The caller's head measures $23\frac{1}{2}$ inches around. What size hat should the Mad Hatter make? _____

2. Kirsi's head measures 61.5 cm in circumference. What size hat does he wear? _____

3. Amanda's head measures $22\frac{3}{8}$ inches in circumference. What hat size does she wear? _____

4. Jel knows that his hat size is $8\frac{1}{2}$. What is the circumference of his head in inches? _____

5. Riel remembers that his hat size is $7\frac{3}{8}$. What is the circumference of his head in centimeters? _____

6. Assume that you have a friend with a very large head, a little larger than size $8\frac{1}{2}$. Determine the next row of the chart to help him out:

   Size _____ ; _____ inches; _____ centimeters.

3. Reading the Nutrition Table

Goal

To read and interpret the information in a "Nutrition Facts" table on a food package.

NCTM Standards Addressed

Standard 2: Mathematics as Communication

Standard 4: Mathematical Connections

Standard 5: Algebra

Standard 6: Functions

Standard 10: Statistics

Teaching Notes

Readers will find discrepancies among nutrition tables. For example, a General Mills™ cereal box suggested that skim milk contains 5% of the minimum daily value of thiamin, while a Shaw's™ box indicated that skim milk has no thiamin. See how many discrepancies students can find. Aside from rounding, which changes several percentages, there are discrepancies in the amount of potassium and vitamin C in milk.

Context

"Nutrition Facts" boxes appear on most food packages. In an increasingly health-conscious nation, students should know how to read them.

Extension Activities

Have students bring in food containers and read labels while learning about nutrition. The school nurse or food-service director will probably be willing to help you discuss healthy eating and nutrition.

Answers

1. There are 220 – 180 = 40 calories in a half-cup of skim milk.

2. There are 55 – 40 = 15 more calories in a half-cup of 1% milk.

3. The RDA of sodium is 2333.33 mg.

4. The RDA of carbohydrates is 293 g.

5. Potassium, Riboflavin, B_{12}, Phosphorus, Magnesium, and Zinc.

6. A half-cup of skim milk contains 15% –6% = 9% of the riboflavin RDA, so you would need to drink just over $5\frac{1}{2}$ cups of skim milk to reach the riboflavin RDA.

7. There is apparently no maximum or minimum daily recommended amount of sugars given by the government.

8. Because amounts in these tables are given in whole numbers, 0 grams could be as much as 499 mg.

Name _____   Date _____

3. Reading the Nutrition Table

Bethany's doctor has advised her to carefully check the ingredients of what she eats. At breakfast this morning, while crunching her cereal, she read the following information from her milk bottle and her cereal box.

Cereal

Nutrition Facts

Serving Size 1 Cup

Amount per Serving	Cereal	with 1/2 cup skim milk
Calories	180	220
Calories from fat	10	10
	% Daily Value	
Total Fat 1g	2%	2%
Saturated Fat 0g	2%	2%
Polyunsaturated Fat 0g		
Monounsaturated Fat 0g		
Cholesterol 0g	0%	1%
Sodium 350mg	15%	17%
Potassium 160mg	5%	10%
Total Carbohydrate 41g	14%	15%
Dietary Fiber 5g	21%	21%
Soluble Fiber 1g		
Sugars 5g		
Other Carbohydrates 31g		
Protein 5g		
Vitamin A	0%	6%
Vitamin C	10%	10%
Calcium	4%	20%
Iron	45%	45%
Thiamin	25%	25%
Riboflavin	6%	15%
Niacin	25%	25%
Vitamin B^6	25%	25%
Folic Acid	25%	25%
Vitamin B^{12}	25%	35%
Vitamin D	0%	25%
Phosphorus	10%	25%
Magnesium	14%	17%
Zinc	20%	21%
Copper	8%	8%

1% Milk

Nutrition Facts

Serving Size 1/2 Cup

Amount per Serving		
Calories		55
Calories from fat		10
		% Daily Value
Total Fat 1250mg		2%
Saturated Fat 750mg		4%
Polyunsaturated		
Monounsaturated Fat		
Cholesterol 8mg		2%
Sodium 63mg		3%
Potassium 0mg		0%
Total Carbohydrate 7g		2%
Dietary Fiber 0 mg		0%
Soluble Fiber 0 mg		0%
Sugars 6g		
Other Carbohydrates 0 mg		
Protein 4g		
Vitamin A		5%
Vitamin C		20%
Calcium		15%
Iron		0%
Thiamin		
Riboflavin		
Niacin		
Vitamin B^6		
Folic Acid		
Vitamin B^{12}		
Vitamin D		25%
Phosphorus		
Magnesium		
Zinc		
Copper		

(continued)

© 1998 J. Weston Walch, Publisher

Real-Life Math: Tables, Charts, and Graphs

3. Reading The Nutrition Table *(continued)*

Answer the following questions that Bethany has about this information:

1. Approximately how many calories are there in a half-cup of skim milk?

_____

2. How many more calories are there in a half-cup of 1% milk than in a half-cup of skim milk?

_____

3. What is the recommended daily allowance of sodium, in milligrams?

_____

4. What is the recommended daily allowance of carbohydrates, in grams?

_____

5. Name three ingredients in milk that are indicated on the cereal box label but not mentioned on the milk label.

_____

6. How many cups of skim milk would you have to drink to get 100% of the daily requirement of riboflavin?

_____

7. Suggest a reason that no percentage is listed on the "Sugars" line of either table.

_____

8. How can the cereal have 0 grams of saturated fat and still contain 2% of the suggested daily value?

_____

4. Stock Quote Tables

Goal

To practice reading tables and learn how to gather information from stock quote tables.

NCTM Standards Addressed

Standard 2: Mathematics as Communication

Standard 4: Mathematical Connections

Standard 5: Algebra

Standard 6: Functions

Standard 10: Statistics

Teaching Notes

The columns of the stock table are: the high and low price of the stock in the past 52 weeks; an abbreviation of the company's name; the symbol that appears on the stock ticker to identify a trade of that stock; last year's dividends paid on the stock ("e" means estimated); the percentage yield that the dividends represent of the current price of the stock; the ratio of the price of the stock per share to the earnings per share reported by the company; the number of shares traded that day in that stock (given in 100's); the high and low price for the previous day; and the last price of a trade from the previous day. The last column represents the change in the price from the previous day's closing price.

Context

The stock tables are full of information and are fairly straightforward, despite looking a bit mystifying. Investment strategies often grow from reading these tables daily and using their information to build financial plans.

Extension Activities

The Dow Jones Company, Standard and Poor's, and other stock investment companies have helpful materials for further study of the stock market. You can also check to see if your state has a stock market game that gives your students imaginary money and allows them to "invest" via the Internet.

Answers

1. National Golf Properties has the ticker symbol TEE.
2. National Semiconductor's 52-week high was $42\frac{7}{8}$.
3. NtlRuralQUICSB has been as low as $24\frac{3}{4}$, and is now trading at $25\frac{3}{4}$.
4. National Semiconductor had 1,354,700 shares change hands, by far the most.
5. NtlHlthInv pf, NtlWstmin pf B, and NtlWstmin pf A are all preferred. They don't have stock ticker symbols either.
6. NtlHlthInv and NtlWstmin had the highest reported dividends.
7. National Oilwell closed the previous session at $1\frac{5}{16}$ more than $26\frac{1}{2}$ or $27\frac{13}{16}$.
8. NtlHlthInv pf never changed from $37\frac{1}{4}$.

4. Stock Quote Tables

Steve Macaluso plans to start buying stocks. He knows that, over time, stocks are a good investment. But before buying, he wants to watch the market for a while, to become familiar with the way it works. he plans to start by reading the stock quote tables in the newspapers.

Steve has found out what some of the headings on the tables mean. The first column, "52-week Hi Lo," shows the highest and lowest prices paid for a share of that stock in the past 52 weeks. The second column, "Stock," gives an abbreviation of the company's name. The third column, "Symbol," shows the symbol that appears on the stock ticker to identify a trade of that stock. The "Div" column gives the dividend paid last year to stockholders; the letter "e" here stands for "estimated." The "Vol" column shows the number of shares of that stock, in hundreds, traded that day. The column headed "Close" shows the price of a stock at the close of the day's trading. The last column, "Net Chng," shows the difference between a stock's price at the close of this day's trading and its price at the close of trading the day before.

The table below is part of a stock quote table. Use it to answer the questions on the next page.

52-Week Hi Lo		Stock	Symbol	Div	Yld	PE	Vol 100's	Hi	Lo	Close	Net Chng
$48^{15}/_{16}$	$39^3/_4$	NtlFuelG	NFG	1.74	3.8	16	938	$46^3/_4$	$45^{13}/_{16}$	46	$-^{13}/_{16}$
35	28	NtlGolfProp	TEE	1.72	5.7	26	225	$30^7/_{86}$	$30^3/_{16}$	$30^5/_{16}$	$-^5/_{16}$
$44^3/_4$	$35^1/_4$	NtlHlthInv	NHI	2.96	7.2	14	236	$41^1/_2$	41	$41^5/_{16}$	$+^5/_{16}$
$39^1/_4$	$31^3/_4$	NtlHlthInv pf		2.13	5.7	...	4	$37^1/_4$	$37^1/_4$	$37^1/_4$	....
$10^1/_2$	$2^1/_8$	NtlMedia	NM		...	dd	4519	$3^1/_4$	$2^5/_8$	$3^1/_{16}$	$+^5/_{16}$
$44^7/_{16}$	14	NtlOilwell	NOI		...	80	996	$27^7/_{16}$	$26^1/_8$	$26^1/_2$	$-1^5/_{16}$
$46^3/_4$	$30^1/_4$	NtlPower	NP	2.32e	5.4	...	62	$43^1/_4$	$42^1/_2$	$42^7/_8$	$-^1/_8$
$44^3/_{16}$	$35^7/_8$	NtlPresto	NPK	2.00	5.0	18	52	$40^3/_{16}$	$39^{11}/_{16}$	$39^7/_8$	...
$12^3/_8$	$6^3/_4$	NtlProc	NAP		...	27	370	$11^7/_{16}$	$11^1/_4$	$11^1/_4$	$-^1/_{16}$
$22^7/_{16}$	$18^7/_8$	NtlPrpnPtnr	NPL	2.10	9.3	...	221	$22^1/_2$	22	$22^1/_2$	$+^1/_4$
$26^7/_{16}$	$24^1/_4$	NtlRuralQUICS	NRU	2.00	7.7	...	18	$26^3/_{16}$	$26^1/_8$	$26^1/_8$	$-^1/_{16}$
$26^1/_{16}$	$24^3/_4$	NtlRuralQUICSB	NRV	.46p	...	...	45	$25^3/_4$	$25^{11}/_{16}$	$25^3/_4$	...
$42^7/_8$	$21^1/_2$	NtlSemi	NSM		...	14	13547	$28^1/_4$	26	$28^1/_8$	$+1^1/_8$
$52^1/_4$	$36^7/_8$	NtlSvcInd	NSI	1.24	2.5	20	649	51	50	50	$+^1/_{16}$
$21^1/_2$	$7^1/_2$	NtlSteel B	NS		...	3	5096	$13^3/_{16}$	$12^9/_{16}$	$12^7/_8$	$+^5/_{16}$
$107^1/_8$	$65^3/_8$	NtlWstmin	NW	3.66e	3.4	...	110	$107^9/_{16}$	$106^3/_{16}$	$106^3/_4$	$+1^1/_4$
$26^9/_{16}$	$24^1/_8$	NtlWstmin pf B		2.19	8.3	...	90	$26^3/_8$	$26^5/_{16}$	$26^3/_8$	$+^1/_{16}$
$27^3/_4$	$24^1/_8$	NtlWstmin pf A		2.66	9.9	...	22	$26^{15}/_{16}$	$26^3/_4$	$26^{15}/_{16}$	$+^1/_8$
$26^9/_{16}$	$23^3/_4$	NtlWstmin XA		1.97	7.6	...	348	$26^1/_4$	$25^{15}/_{16}$	26	$+^1/_8$
$27^1/_4$	24	NtlWstmin C		2.16	8.0	...	133	$27^1/_8$	$26^3/_4$	27	...

4. Stock Quote Tables (continued)

1. What is the ticker symbol for National Golf Properties? _____

2. What is the highest price anyone has paid for National Semiconductor stock in the last 52 weeks?

   _____

3. None of these stocks set new lows for their price in the last 52 weeks, but one stock is exactly one dollar per share above its 52-week low. Which one is it? _____

4. Which stock had the most shares traded? How many shares? _____

   _____

5. "Preferred" stocks have a "pf" in their names. What preferred stocks appear here, and what other fact do you observe about their table entries?

   _____

   _____

6. Of all the dividends reported, which two are the highest in value? _____

   _____

7. At what price did National Oilwell close in the previous trading session? _____

8. Which stock's price remained unchanged for the trading session identified here?

   _____

 Real-Life Math: Tables, Charts, and Graphs

5. Tax Tables

Goal

To practice reading tables using IRS tax tables.

NCTM Standards Addressed

Standard 2: Mathematics as Communication

Standard 4: Mathematical Connections

Standard 5: Algebra

Standard 6: Functions

Standard 10: Statistics

Teaching Notes

Reading these tables can be turned into a more challenging mathematical activity if you ask students to calculate the rates being charged. The portion of the tax tables shown includes the income values above *and* below the cutoff where single-income taxpayers switch from the 15 percent bracket to the 28 percent bracket. Most students don't know about graduated rates, and this gives them a good opportunity to brainstorm about it.

Context

Filling out tax forms is a chore for most people. One part of this process is calculating how much tax you owe, based on your adjusted income.

Extension Activities

- Contact your local IRS office to obtain complete copies of the current year's tax tables.

- The IRS publishes a useful series about taxes, which is available free. It addresses tax law, taxation theory, introduces new forms, and gives students practice with forms that they are already filling out if they are in the job market. An update is mailed each year, including videos, software, forms, and teaching materials.

Answers

1. The single person would pay $3,521.

2. The head of household would pay $4,616.

3. The married couple would pay $4,181.

4. Your income range would have been $31,300 to $31,350.

5. Your income range would be $31,550 to $31,600.

6. The changeover comes at $24,700.

7. The single person would pay $24,700 \times .15 + $27,300 \times .28 = $11,349$.

5. Tax Tables

Judson Ward-Chene is an accountant, specializing in taxes. Each year, he sits down with clients and helps them figure out what information they need to calculate their adjusted income (the income on which they will be taxed). After they have figured out their adjusted income, they need to calculate how much they have already paid (through deductions), and how much they owe. The booklet that the IRS sends out has tables that help you calculate your tax. Some of the tables appear on page 14. Can you help Doug answer the following questions?

1. How much tax would a single person have to pay on an adjusted income of $23,458?

    _____

2. How much tax would a head of a household have to pay on an adjusted income of $30,776?

    _____

3. How much tax would a married couple filing jointly have to pay on an adjusted income of $27,892?

    _____

4. If you are single and owe $5,567 in income tax, what was your income range for the year covered in the table?

    _____

5. If you are married filing jointly and owe $4,736 in income tax, what was your income range for the year covered in the table?

    _____

6. Our tax code is tiered—that is, it uses different tax rates for different levels of income. For a married couple filing jointly making less than $41,150, a tax of 15 percent is imposed. For every dollar earned above $41,150, a tax of 28 percent is imposed. You can see this in the change in the increments of increase in the table. How much can a single person make before they cross from the 15 percent to the 28 percent category?

    _____

7. Given what you know about the two tiers of the tax code and the tables on page 14, how much tax would a single person earning $52,000 owe?

    _____

(continued)

5. Tax Tables *(continued)*

1997 Tax Table—Continued

If line 38 (taxable income) is— At least	But less than	Single	Married filing jointly*	Married filing separately	Head of a household	If line 38 (taxable income) is— At least	But less than	Single	Married filing jointly*	Married filing separately	Head of a household	If line 38 (taxable income) is— At least	But less than	Single	Married filing jointly*	Married filing separately	Head of a household
23,000						**26,000**						**29,000**					
23,000	23,050	3,454	3,454	3,769	3,454	26,000	26,050	4,083	3,904	4,609	3,904	29,000	29,050	4,923	4,354	5,449	4,354
23,050	23,100	3,461	3,461	3,783	3,461	26,050	26,100	4,097	3,911	4,623	3,911	29,050	29,100	4,937	4,361	5,463	4,361
23,100	23,150	3,469	3,469	3,797	3,469	26,100	26,150	4,111	3,919	4,637	3,919	29,100	29,150	4,951	4,369	5,477	4,369
23,150	23,200	3,476	3,476	3,811	3,476	26,150	26,200	4,125	3,926	4,651	3,926	29,150	29,200	4,965	4,376	5,491	4,376
23,200	23,250	3,484	3,484	3,825	3,484	26,200	26,250	4,139	3,934	4,665	3,934	29,200	29,250	4,979	4,384	5,505	4,384
23,250	23,300	3,491	3,491	3,839	3,491	26,250	26,300	4,153	3,941	4,679	3,941	29,250	29,300	4,993	4,391	5,519	4,391
23,300	23,350	3,499	3,499	3,853	3,499	26,300	26,350	4,167	3,949	4,693	3,949	29,300	29,350	5,007	4,399	5,533	4,399
23,350	23,400	3,506	3,506	3,867	3,506	26,350	26,400	4,181	3,956	4,707	3,956	29,350	29,400	5,021	4,406	5,547	4,406
23,400	23,450	3,514	3,514	3,881	3,514	26,400	26,450	4,195	3,964	4,721	3,964	29,400	29,450	5,035	4,414	5,561	4,414
23,450	23,500	3,521	3,521	3,895	3,521	26,450	26,500	4,209	3,971	4,735	3,971	29,450	29,500	5,049	4,421	5,575	4,421
23,500	23,550	3,529	3,529	3,909	3,529	26,500	26,550	4,223	3,979	4,749	3,979	29,500	29,550	5,063	4,429	5,589	4,429
23,550	23,600	3,536	3,536	3,923	3,536	26,550	26,600	4,237	3,986	4,763	3,986	29,550	29,600	5,077	4,436	5,603	4,436
23,600	23,650	3,544	3,544	3,937	3,544	26,600	26,650	4,251	3,994	4,777	3,994	29,600	29,650	5,091	4,444	5,617	4,444
23,650	23,700	3,551	3,551	3,951	3,551	26,650	26,700	4,265	4,001	4,791	4,001	29,650	29,700	5,105	4,451	5,631	4,451
23,700	23,750	3,559	3,559	3,965	3,559	26,700	26,750	4,279	4,009	4,805	4,009	29,700	29,750	5,119	4,459	5,645	4,459
23,750	23,800	3,566	3,566	3,979	3,566	26,750	26,800	4,293	4,016	4,819	4,016	29,750	29,800	5,133	4,466	5,659	4,466
23,800	23,850	3,574	3,574	3,993	3,574	26,800	26,850	4,307	4,024	4,833	4,024	29,800	29,850	5,147	4,474	5,673	4,474
23,850	23,900	3,581	3,581	4,007	3,581	26,850	26,900	4,321	4,031	4,847	4,031	29,850	29,900	5,161	4,481	5,687	4,481
23,900	23,950	3,589	3,589	4,021	3,589	26,900	26,950	4,335	4,039	4,861	4,039	29,900	29,950	5,175	4,489	5,701	4,489
23,950	24,000	3,596	3,596	4,035	3,596	26,950	27,000	4,349	4,046	4,875	4,046	29,950	30,000	5,189	4,496	5,715	4,496
24,000						**27,000**						**30,000**					
24,000	24,050	3,604	3,604	4,049	3,604	27,000	27,050	4,363	4,054	4,889	4,054	30,000	30,050	5,203	4,504	5,729	4,504
24,050	24,100	3,611	3,611	4,063	3,611	27,050	27,100	4,377	4,061	4,903	4,061	30,050	30,100	5,217	4,511	5,743	4,511
24,100	24,150	3,619	3,619	4,077	3,619	27,100	27,150	4,391	4,069	4,917	4,069	30,100	30,150	5,231	4,519	5,757	4,519
24,150	24,200	3,626	3,626	4,091	3,626	27,150	27,200	4,405	4,076	4,931	4,076	30,150	30,200	5,245	4,526	5,771	4,526
24,200	24,250	3,634	3,634	4,105	3,634	27,200	27,250	4,419	4,084	4,945	4,084	30,200	30,250	5,259	4,534	5,785	4,534
24,250	24,300	3,641	3,641	4,119	3,641	27,250	27,300	4,433	4,091	4,959	4,091	30,250	30,300	5,273	4,541	5,799	4,541
24,300	24,350	3,649	3,649	4,133	3,649	27,300	27,350	4,447	4,099	4,973	4,099	30,300	30,350	5,287	4,549	5,813	4,549
24,350	24,400	3,656	3,656	4,147	3,656	27,350	27,400	4,461	4,106	4,987	4,106	30,350	30,400	5,301	4,556	5,827	4,556
24,400	24,450	3,664	3,664	4,161	3,664	27,400	27,450	4,475	4,114	5,001	4,114	30,400	30,450	5,315	4,564	5,841	4,564
24,450	24,500	3,671	3,671	4,175	3,671	27,450	27,500	4,489	4,121	5,015	4,121	30,450	30,500	5,329	4,571	5,855	4,571
24,500	24,550	3,679	3,679	4,189	3,679	27,500	27,550	4,503	4,129	5,029	4,129	30,500	30,550	5,343	4,579	5,869	4,579
24,550	24,600	3,686	3,686	4,203	3,686	27,550	27,600	4,517	4,136	5,043	4,136	30,550	30,600	5,357	4,586	5,883	4,586
24,600	24,650	3,694	3,694	4,217	3,694	27,600	27,650	4,531	4,144	5,057	4,144	30,600	30,650	5,371	4,594	5,897	4,594
24,650	24,700	3,705	3,701	4,231	3,701	27,650	27,700	4,545	4,151	5,071	4,151	30,650	30,700	5,385	4,601	5,911	4,601
24,700	24,750	3,719	3,709	4,245	3,709	27,700	27,750	4,559	4,159	5,085	4,159	30,700	30,750	5,399	4,609	5,925	4,609
24,750	24,800	3,733	3,716	4,259	3,716	27,750	27,800	4,573	4,166	5,099	4,166	30,750	30,800	5,413	4,616	5,939	4,616
24,800	24,850	3,747	3,724	4,273	3,724	27,800	27,850	4,587	4,174	5,113	4,174	30,800	30,850	5,427	4,624	5,953	4,624
24,850	24,900	3,761	3,731	4,287	3,731	27,850	27,900	4,601	4,181	5,127	4,181	30,850	30,900	5,441	4,631	5,967	4,631
24,900	24,950	3,775	3,739	4,301	3,739	27,900	27,950	4,615	4,189	5,141	4,189	30,900	30,950	5,455	4,639	5,981	4,639
24,950	25,000	3,789	3,746	4,315	3,746	27,950	28,000	4,629	4,196	5,155	4,196	30,950	31,000	5,469	4,646	5,995	4,646
25,000						**28,000**						**31,000**					
25,000	25,050	3,803	3,754	4,329	3,754	28,000	28,050	4,643	4,204	5,169	4,204	31,000	31,050	5,483	4,654	6,009	4,654
25,050	25,100	3,817	3,761	4,343	3,761	28,050	28,100	4,657	4,211	5,183	4,211	31,050	31,100	5,497	4,661	6,023	4,661
25,100	25,150	3,831	3,769	4,357	3,769	28,100	28,150	4,671	4,219	5,197	4,219	31,100	31,150	5,511	4,669	6,037	4,669
25,150	25,200	3,845	3,776	4,371	3,776	28,150	28,200	4,685	4,226	5,211	4,226	31,150	31,200	5,525	4,676	6,051	4,676
25,200	25,250	3,859	3,784	4,385	3,784	28,200	28,250	4,699	4,234	5,225	4,234	31,200	31,250	5,539	4,684	6,065	4,684
25,250	25,300	3,873	3,791	4,399	3,791	28,250	28,300	4,713	4,241	5,239	4,241	31,250	31,300	5,553	4,691	6,079	4,691
25,300	25,350	3,887	3,799	4,413	3,799	28,300	28,350	4,727	4,249	5,253	4,249	31,300	31,350	5,567	4,699	6,093	4,699
25,350	25,400	3,901	3,806	4,427	3,806	28,350	28,400	4,741	4,256	5,267	4,256	31,350	31,400	5,581	4,706	6,107	4,706
25,400	25,450	3,915	3,814	4,441	3,814	28,400	28,450	4,755	4,264	5,281	4,264	31,400	31,450	5,595	4,714	6,121	4,714
25,450	25,500	3,929	3,821	4,455	3,821	28,450	28,500	4,769	4,271	5,295	4,271	31,450	31,500	5,609	4,721	6,135	4,721
25,500	25,550	3,943	3,829	4,469	3,829	28,500	28,550	4,783	4,279	5,309	4,279	31,500	31,550	5,623	4,729	6,149	4,729
25,550	25,600	3,957	3,836	4,483	3,836	28,550	28,600	4,797	4,286	5,323	4,286	31,550	31,600	5,637	4,736	6,163	4,736
25,600	25,650	3,971	3,844	4,497	3,844	28,600	28,650	4,811	4,294	5,337	4,294	31,600	31,650	5,651	4,744	6,177	4,744
25,650	25,700	3,985	3,851	4,511	3,851	28,650	28,700	4,825	4,301	5,351	4,301	31,650	31,700	5,665	4,751	6,191	4,751
25,700	25,750	3,999	3,859	4,525	3,859	28,700	28,750	4,839	4,309	5,365	4,309	31,700	31,750	5,679	4,759	6,205	4,759
25,750	25,800	4,013	3,866	4,539	3,866	28,750	28,800	4,853	4,316	5,379	4,316	31,750	31,800	5,693	4,766	6,219	4,766
25,800	25,850	4,027	3,874	4,553	3,874	28,800	28,850	4,867	4,324	5,393	4,324	31,800	31,850	5,707	4,774	6,233	4,774
25,850	25,900	4,041	3,881	4,567	3,881	28,850	28,900	4,881	4,331	5,407	4,331	31,850	31,900	5,721	4,781	6,247	4,781
25,900	25,950	4,055	3,889	4,581	3,889	28,900	28,950	4,895	4,339	5,421	4,339	31,900	31,950	5,735	4,789	6,261	4,789
25,950	26,000	4,069	3,896	4,595	3,896	28,950	29,000	4,909	4,346	5,435	4,346	31,950	32,000	5,749	4,796	6,275	4,796

* This column must also be used by a qualifying widow(er).

Continued on next page

6. Lumber Inventory

Goal

To practice reading tables on the availability of inventory in a lumber yard.

NCTM Standards Addressed

Standard 2: Mathematics as Communication

Standard 4: Mathematical Connections

Standard 5: Algebra

Standard 6: Functions

Standard 10: Statistics

Teaching Notes

Charts with titles on both the columns and the rows can give you information only about two factors. However, if you include additional information *in* the cells of the table, you have augmented the table. In this case, the rows of the table represent cut dimensions, the columns represent lengths, and the cells contain further information about quality and price.

Context

As any home handyperson can tell you, a huge variety of cuts of wood is available, both in size and in quality. Choosing affordable cuts of the right quality can be a challenge.

Extension Activities

Encourage students to find similar charts in newspaper advertisements and break down the information they find.

Answers

1. The 2" × 8" lengths available are 8 feet, 10 feet, and 12 feet.

2. The most common lumber length appears to be 8 feet.

3. It will cost Jerall $37.56 to buy four 10-foot lengths of 2" × 4" (prime).

4. It would cost Jerall $73.90 to buy ten 8-foot lengths of 2" × 6" (first).

5. It would cost Jerall $67.33 to buy six 12-foot lengths and one 8-foot length of 2" × 6" (first). His savings would be $6.57.

6. The least expensive way is for Jerall to buy four 10-foot lengths and two 8-foot lengths, costing $58.74.

7. Answers will vary. The obvious answer is that a blank represents a size of wood not available. Some students will speculate as to *why* it is not available, i.e.: "The 1" × 2" would break if it was as much as 12 feet long" or "Since so many people want to use 2" × 10"s as a long structure piece, no one would buy a 4-foot long 2" × 10"."

6. Lumber Inventory

Jerall Kane has decided to build a deck onto his house. He isn't sure of the design, but he has found a local lumber yard that has reasonable prices. He visited the lumberyard and came home with a circular advertising their current prices on various types of wood and various lengths. The information is included in the following table. Can you help Jerall price out his selections?

Length × Type	4'	6'	8'	10'	12'
1" × 2"	FIRST—$1.29	FIRST— $1.89	FIRST— $2.39 PRIME— $3.59	FIRST— $2.79 PRIME— $3.89	
1" × 3"	FIRST—$1.59	FIRST— $2.29	FIRST— $2.99 PRIME— $3.89	FIRST— $3.59 PRIME— $4.89	
2" × 4"	FIRST—$3.89	FIRST— $4.99 PRIME—$6.59	FIRST— $6.49 PRIME— $8.59	FIRST— $7.69 PRIME— $9.39	
2" × 6"		FIRST— $5.89 PRIME—$7.59	FIRST— $7.39 PRIME— $9.29	FIRST— $8.89 PRIME—$11.19	FIRST— $9.99
2" × 8"			FIRST— $8.59 PRIME—$10.09	FIRST— $10.69 PRIME—$12.59	FIRST—$11.19
2" × 10"			FIRST— $9.49 PRIME—$11.69	FIRST— $11.79 PRIME—$14.19	FIRST—$13.19
2" × 12"			FIRST— $11.79 PRIME—$14.59	FIRST— $14.19 PRIME—$16.99	FIRST—$16.29
4" × 4"		FIRST— $6.89	FIRST— $8.99	FIRST— $10.19	FIRST—$12.89
4" × 6"		FIRST— $7.99	FIRST— $9.99		

(continued)

© 1998 J. Weston Walch, Publisher   *Real-Life Math: Tables, Charts, and Graphs*

6. Lumber Inventory *(continued)*

1. What lengths of 2" × 8" are available for Jerall to buy?

   _____

   _____

2. Judging from this chart, what is the most common length of lumber available?

   _____

3. Jerall needs 40 feet of 2" × 4" (prime) for his railings. How much will it cost him if he buys four 10-foot lengths?

   _____

4. Jerall figures he needs twenty 2" × 6" 4-foot pieces for his frame. It can be first quality instead of prime, because no one will see it. How much would it cost Jerall to buy ten 8-foot pieces and cut each of them in half?

   _____

5. How much would Jerall save if he bought six 12-foot long 2" × 6" and one 8-foot 2" × 6" instead?

   _____

6. Jerall needs four 6-foot long 4" × 4" posts and eight 4-foot long 4" × 4" posts. What is the least expensive way for him to buy the wood, assuming he can cut it accurately?

   _____

7. Many of the squares in the table on page 16 are blank. Speculate as to why.

   _____

7. Box Scores

Goal

To learn about reading tables in the context of baseball box scores.

NCTM Standards Addressed

Standard 2: Mathematics as Communication

Standard 4: Mathematical Connections

Standard 5: Algebra

Standard 6: Functions

Standard 10: Statistics

Teaching Notes

A box score is a table with several parts. At the top, it gives the score. Next come the individual hitting statistics for each player. The home team is always listed on the right. Next is an inning-by-inning line score. In the game shown in the box score on the student page, the "X" on the bottom of the final inning means that Florida didn't bat that inning. After Cleveland's last at-bat, the score was 7 to 4, with the Florida Marlins the clear winners. Other information about individual plays follows. Next is the pitching box. Below that box is additional information about pitching. Finally, the umpires, time of the game, and attendance are listed.

Context

Baseball box scores are easy to find and contain much information. Students may be better able to follow a local team if they can read a box score.

Extension Activities

From late March to October, box scores appear daily in the paper. Have students bring some in and, when they are familiar with them, suggest changes that would give the reader even more information about the game.

Answers

1. Marlins 7, Indians 4.
2. The Marlins were the home team.
3. Omar Vizquel was 0 for 4.
4. Yes. Johnson drove in one run.
5. The Indians struck out 10 times in the game.
6. Livan Hernandez pitched $5\frac{2}{3}$ innings, the most of any pitcher.
7. Gary Sheffield made the only error.
8. The most runs were scored in the fourth inning, when the Marlins scored four runs.
9. Four players had two hits: Roberts, Justice, Grissom, and Bonilla.
10. Three pinch hitters: Branson and Giles for the Indians and Cangelosi for the Marlins.

7. Box Scores

Over the years, professional sports and the news media have developed efficient ways of communicating more information about a game than just the score. Perhaps the most information about a game can be found in a baseball "box score." See if you can find the information requested in the following box score of Game 1 in the 1997 World Series between the Florida Marlins and the Cleveland Indians.

①

MARLINS 7, INDIANS 4

②

Cleveland	AB	R	H	RBI	BB	K		Florida	AB	R	H	RBI	BB	K
Roberts 2B	4	1	2	0	1	0		White CF	4	0	0	0	1	1
Vizquel SS	4	0	0	0	0	2	③	Renteria SS	4	0	0	1	0	0
Ramirez RF	3	1	1	1	2	0		Sheffield RF	2	1	0	0	2	1
Justice LF	4	0	2	1	1	0		Bonilla 3B	3	2	2	0	1	1
Williams 3B	5	0	1	0	0	1		Daulton 1B	2	1	1	0	0	0
Thome 1B	5	1	1	1	0	2		Conine 1B	2	0	1	1	0	0
Alomar C	5	0	1	0	0	2		Alou CF	3	1	1	3	1	1
Grissom CF	3	1	2	0	1	1		Johnson C	3	1	1	1	1	0
Hershiser P	2	0	0	0	0	1		Counsell 2B	3	1	1	0	1	0
Juden P	0	0	0	0	0	0		Hernandez P	2	0	0	0	0	0
Branson PH	1	0	0	0	0	1		Cook P	0	0	0	0	0	0
Plunk P	0	0	0	0	0	0		Powell P	0	0	0	0	0	0
Giles PH	1	0	1	1	0	0		Cangelosi PH	1	0	0	0	0	1
Assenmacher P	0	0	0	0	0	0		Nen P	0	0	0	0	0	0
Totals	37	4	11	1	5	10		Totals	29	7	7	6	7	5

④

CLEVELAND 100 011 010—4
FLORIDA   011 420 00x—7

⑤ **E** - Sheffield (1). **DP** - Cleveland 1. **LOB** - Cleveland 12, Florida 6. **2B** - Counsell (1), Roberts 2 (2), Grissom (10), Giles (1). **HR** - Alou (1), Johnson (1), Ramirez (1), Thome (1). **S** - Hernandez, Visquel.

⑥

	IP	H	R	ER	BB	K
Cleveland						
Hershiser L	4 1/3	6	7	7	4	2
Juden	2/3	0	0	0	2	0
Plunk	2	1	0	0	1	1
Assenmacher	1	0	0	0	0	2
Florida						
Hernandez W	5 2/3	8	3	3	2	5
Cook	1 2/3	0	0	0	1	2
Powell	2/3	1	1	1	2	1
Nen S	1	2	0	0	0	2

⑦ **WP** - Juden

⑧ **Umpires: H -** Montague, **1b -** Ford, **2b -** West, **3b -** Kosc, **LF -** Marsh, **RF -** Kaiser.

⑨ **T -** 3:19. **A -** 67,245.

Key to baseball box score

1 Final score	6 Pitching box
2 Visiting team on the left, home team on the right	L—loss W—win
3 Individual player hitting statistics	S—save IP—innings pitched
AB—at bats R—runs scored	H—hits R—runs allowed
H—hits RBI—runs batted in	ER—earned runs allowed
BB—walks K—strikeouts	BB—walks K—strikeouts
4 Inning-by-inning line score	7 Details about pitches
5 Details about individual plays	WP—wild pitch PB—passed ball
E—errors DP—double plays	8 Umpires
LOB—runners left on base at end of inning	9 T—time of game A—attendance
SB—stolen bases 2B—doubles	
3B—triples HR—home runs	
S—sacrifice bunts SF—sacrifice flies	

(continued)

7. Box Scores *(continued)*

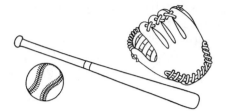

1. What was the final score of the game?

   _____

2. Who was the home team?

   _____

3. One player for the Indians had no hits in four at-bats. Who was he?

   _____

4. Did Charles Johnson, the Marlins all-star catcher, drive in any runs? If so, how many?

   _____

5. How many times did Indians batters strike out in the game?

   _____

6. Which pitcher pitched the most innings in the game?

   _____

7. Who made an error in the game?

   _____

8. In what inning were the most runs scored?

   _____

9. How many players managed two hits in the game and who were they?

   _____

10. How many pinch hitters were used in the game?

   _____

8. Making a Nutrition Table

Goal

To create a "Nutrition Facts" table on a food package given the pertinent information.

NCTM Standards Addressed

Standard 1: Mathematics as Problem Solving

Standard 2: Mathematics as Communication

Standard 4: Mathematical Connections

Standard 5: Algebra

Standard 6: Functions

Standard 10: Statistics

Teaching Notes

Readers will find discrepancies among nutrition tables. For example, a General Mills cereal box suggested that skim milk contains 5% of the minimum daily value of thiamin, while a Shaw's box indicated that skim milk has no thiamin. See how many discrepancies the students can find. Aside from rounding, which changes several percentages, there are discrepancies in the amount of vitamin A and vitamin C in milk.

Context

"Nutrition Facts" boxes appear on most food packages. In an increasingly health-conscious nation, students should know how to read them.

Extension Activities

Have students bring in containers and read labels while learning about nutrition. The school nurse or food-service director will probably be willing to help you discuss healthy eating and nutrition.

Answers

Cereal

Nutrition Facts
Serving Size 1 cup

Amount per Serving	Cereal	with 1/2 cup skim milk	with 1/2 cup 1% milk
Calories	180	220	235
Calories from fat	10	10	20
	% Daily Value		
Total Fat 1g	2%	2%	4%
Saturated Fat 0g	2%	2%	6%
Polyunsaturated Fat 0g			0%
Monounsaturated Fat 0g			0%
Cholesterol 0g	0%	1%	2%
Sodium 420mg	18%	20%	21%
Potassium 200mg	6%	11%	11%
Total Carbohydrate 41g	14%	15%	16%
Dietary Fiber 5g	21%	21%	21%
Soluble Fiber 1g			
Sugars 5g			
Other Carbohydrates 31g			
Protein 5g			
Vitamin A	0%	6%	5%
Vitamin C	10%	10%	12%
Calcium	4%	20%	19%
Iron	45%	45%	45%
Thiamin	25%	25%	25%
Riboflavin	6%	15%	6%
Niacin	25%	25%	25%
Vitamin B^6	25%	25%	25%
Folic Acid	25%	25%	25%
Vitamin B^{12}	25%	35%	35%
Vitamin D	0%	25%	25%
Phosphorus	10%	25%	25%
Magnesium	14%	17%	18%
Zinc	20%	21%	20%
Copper	8%	8%	8%

8. Making a Nutrition Table

Megan works for a cereal company. She is responsible for making sure that the information on the package is accurate. The company has decided to change its "Nutrition Facts" table to include how the nutrition changes if 1% milk is used instead of skim milk. Using the tables below, can you help Megan by filling in the blanks in the table on the next page.

Cereal

Nutrition Facts
Serving Size 1 cup

Amount per Serving	Cereal	with 1/2 cup skim milk
Calories	180	220
Calories from fat	10	10
	% Daily Value	
Total Fat 1g	2%	2%
Saturated Fat 0g	2%	2%
Polyunsaturated Fat 0g		
Monounsaturated Fat 0g		
Cholesterol 0g	0%	1%
Sodium 420mg	18%	20%
Potassium 200mg	6%	11%
Total Carbohydrate 41g	14%	15%
Dietary Fiber 5g	21%	21%
Soluble Fiber 1g		
Sugars 5g		
Other Carbohydrates 31g		
Protein 5g		
Vitamin A	0%	6%
Vitamin C	10%	10%
Calcium	4%	20%
Iron	45%	45%
Thiamin	25%	25%
Riboflavin	6%	15%
Niacin	25%	25%
Vitamin B^6	25%	25%
Folic Acid	25%	25%
Vitamin B^{12}	25%	35%
Vitamin D	0%	25%
Phosphorus	10%	25%
Magnesium	14%	17%
Zinc	20%	21%
Copper	8%	8%

1% Milk

Nutrition Facts
Serving Size 1/2 cup

Amount per Serving		% Daily Value
Calories	55	
Calories from fat	10	
		% Daily Value
Total Fat 1250mg		2%
Saturated Fat 750mg		4%
Polyunsaturated		
Monounsaturated Fat		
Cholesterol 8mg		2%
Sodium 630mg		3%
Potassium 167mg		5%
Total Carbohydrate 7g		2%
Dietary Fiber 0mg		0%
Soluble Fiber 0mg		0%
Sugars 6g		
Other Carbohydrates 0mg		0%
Protein 4g		
Vitamin A		5%
Vitamin C		2%
Calcium		15%
Iron		0%
Thiamin		
Riboflavin		
Niacin		
Vitamin B^6		
Folic Acid		
Vitamin B^{12}		10%
Vitamin D		25%
Phosphorus		15%
Magnesium		4%
Zinc		
Copper		

(continued)

8. Making a Nutrition Table (continued)

Nutrition Facts

Serving Size 1 cup

Amount per Serving	Cereal	with 1/2 cup skim milk	with 1/2 cup 1% milk
Calories	180	220	
Calories from fat	10	10	
	% Daily Value		
Total Fat 1g	2%	2%	
Saturated Fat 0g	2%	2%	
Polyunsaturated Fat 0g			
Monounsaturated Fat 0g			
Cholesterol 0g	0%	1%	
Sodium 420mg	18%	20%	
Potassium 200mg	6%	11%	
Total Carbohydrate 41g	14%	15%	
Dietary Fiber 5g	21%	21%	
Soluble Fiber 1g			
Sugars 5g			
Other Carbohydrates 31g			
Protein 5g			
Vitamin A	0%	6%	
Vitamin C	10%	10%	
Calcium	4%	20%	
Iron	45%	45%	
Thiamin	25%	25%	
Riboflavin	6%	15%	
Niacin	25%	25%	
Vitamin B^6	25%	25%	
Folic Acid	25%	25%	
Vitamin B^{12}	25%	35%	
Vitamin D	0%	25%	
Phosphorus	10%	25%	
Magnesium	14%	17%	
Zinc	20%	21%	
Copper	8%	8%	

9. Creating Tax Tables

Goal

To allow students to create a table of information about tax rates that they can then interpret.

NCTM Standards Addressed

Standard 1: Mathematics as Problem Solving

Standard 2: Mathematics as Communication

Standard 4: Mathematical Connections

Standard 5: Algebra

Standard 6: Functions

Standard 10: Statistics

Teaching Notes

The calculations involved in preparing this form are straightforward. However, the comparisons are more sophisticated. You may get a range of answers to that part of the worksheet.

Context

Tax reform is a political hot potato. Every new proposal is immediately evaluated on the basis of who will pay more and who will pay less. This kind of cursory analysis is only a start in evaluating changes to tax code.

Extension Activities

You may want to discuss the difference between graduated taxes, such as the current and proposed tax plans, and flat taxes, such as the plan proposed by 1996 presidential candidate Steven Forbes. Ask students to design their own tax plan and investigate what it would do to tax collections and the budget deficit/surplus.

Answers to Worksheet

Income	Current Tax	New Tax Plan
$10,000	$1,504	0
$20,000	$3,004	$2,200
$30,000	$5,203	$4,700
$40,000	$8,003	$7,500
$50,000	$10,803	$10,600
$60,000	$13,611	$13,900
$70,000	$16,711	$17,400
$80,000	$19,811	$20,900
$90,000	$22,911	$24,400
$100,000	$26,010	$27,900

Name _____   Date _____

9. Creating Tax Tables

Lori Norman is an employee in a senatorial office in Washington, DC. She has been asked to create a new tax table so that the senator can compare the current tax table with a new way of calculating taxes. The senator wants a comparison of tax bills for families who earn $10,000 to $100,000 per year, in increments of $10,000. The new calculation strategy is that the government would not tax anyone for the first $10,000 they make. Taxpayers would be taxed 22% of the second $10,000, 25% of the third $10,000, 28% of the next $10,000, 31% of the next $10,000, 33% of the next $10,000, and 35% of any amount above $60,000. Below is the tax table with the current taxation amounts. Fill out the new plan column. Then compare the two plans for various households.

Income	Current Tax Plan	New Tax Plan
$10,000	$1,504	
$20,000	$3,004	
$30,000	$5,203	
$40,000	$8,003	
$50,000	$10,803	
$60,000	$13,611	
$70,000	$16,711	
$80,000	$19,811	
$90,000	$22,911	
$100,000	$26,010	

Comparison: _____

_____

_____

_____

_____

10. Postal Rates

Goal

To create a simple table in the context of postal rates and office work.

NCTM Standards Addressed

Standard 1: Mathematics as Problem Solving

Standard 2: Mathematics as Communication

Standard 4: Mathematical Connections

Standard 5: Algebra

Standard 6: Functions

Standard 10: Statistics

Teaching Notes

This step table is fairly simple to create. Students only need to add 23 cents to each previous entry. However, as an introduction to simple linear functions, you may want to ask them to write a function for the cost, such as would be plugged into a spreadsheet.

Context

Postal rates change frequently, and new tables for mail costs need to be generated. Heavy turnover and frequent retraining are common in these types of job settings, and accurate tables and graphs often ease the jobs of supervisors.

Extension Activities

Have students anticipate future postal cost increases and regenerate this table. Consider the possibility that when a package exceeds a certain size, the nature of the table changes.

Answers

Weight (oz)	Price
1.0	$0.39
2.0	$0.62
3.0	$0.85
4.0	$1.08
5.0	$1.31
6.0	$1.54
7.0	$1.77
8.0	$2.00
9.0	$2.23
10.0	$2.46
11.0	$2.69
12.0	$2.92
13.0	$3.15
14.0	$3.38
15.0	$3.61
16.0	$3.84
17.0	$4.07
18.0	$4.30
19.0	$4.53
20.0	$4.76
21.0	$4.99
22.0	$5.22

10. Postal Rates

Tonya LaChance runs the mail room of a large company. Unfortunately, the company is not willing to invest much money in salaries for her employees, so they don't stick around very long. Consequently, Tonya often has to train new employees. One skill they must learn is using the mail machine. The employee must weigh the mail on a scale next to the machine and then decide how much postage to put on each package. Tonya has decided that it would be easier to have a chart of the prices for various weights. Right now first-class mail in the United States costs $0.39 for the first ounce and $0.23 for every ounce thereafter. Can you help Tonya create her table?

Weight in ounces	Price
1.0	

© 1998 J. Weston Walch, Publisher   *Real-Life Math: Tables, Charts, and Graphs*

11. Loan Payments

Goal

To create a table that will be useful in calculating monthly loan payments.

NCTM Standards Addressed

Standard 1: Mathematics as Problem Solving

Standard 2: Mathematics as Communication

Standard 4: Mathematical Connections

Standard 5: Algebra

Standard 6: Functions

Standard 10: Statistics

Teaching Notes

Once students understand that the payments in the first table are per $1,000, and that they must multiply these figures by the number of thousands of dollars in the loan, they should find creating this table straightforward. From there, you can lead students to a critical analysis of the figures in the table they develop. In terms of monthly payments, the 30-year loan at 7% may look like the best option, but if students multiply the monthly payment by the total number of payments, they will see that the 15-year loan actually costs far less than the 30-year loan (1078 × 180 = 194,040 as opposed to 798 × 360 = 287,280).

Context

When considering loans, many consumers are concerned with the size of their monthly payments rather than the size of the loan. Loan payment tables come in handy in considering what the monthly payments will be.

Extension Activities

- Have students use the information in the tables to think of ways to minimize the cost of borrowing money, e.g., if the borrower can put down $15,000 more in a downpayment on a 15-year loan at 7 percent, the total amount repaid will be $169,911, for a savings of $9,129 in interest over the life of the loan.

- Many spreadsheet programs will prepare an amortization schedule for a loan, showing what the monthly payments would be and how much of each payment goes to paying the principal and how much goes to pay the interest on the loan.

- Your local bank or credit union would probably be willing to send a representative to discuss loans and repayment schedules with your students.

Answers

Monthly payments on a loan of $120,000

	15 years	20 years	25 years	30 years
7%	$1078.80	$930.00	$848.40	$798.00
8%	$1147.20	$1003.20	$926.40	$880.80
9%	$1216.80	$1080.00	$1006.80	$966.00
10%	$1290.00	$1158.00	$1090.80	$1053.60
11%	$1364.40	$1238.40	$1176.00	$1142.40

11. Loan Payments

If you wanted to buy a house, how would you pay for it? Most people can't pay for a new house with cash. They save as much as they can, then borrow the rest of the money from a bank. This loan is paid back in equal monthly payments over a period of years. Part of each payment goes to cover the interest on the loan. This is the cost to the borrower of borrowing the money. The table below shows the monthly payments per thousand dollars at various interest rates for different loan periods. If the original loan amount was $10,000, you would multiply each payment by 10 to find out what your loan payments would be. For example, if you borrowed $10,000 for 15 years at 7 percent interest, you would pay $89.90 ($8.99 × 10) every month for 15 years.

Monthly payments per $1,000 borrowed

	15 years	20 years	25 years	30 years
7%	$8.99	$7.75	$7.07	$6.65
8%	$9.56	$8.36	$7.72	$7.34
9%	$10.14	$9.00	$8.39	$8.05
10%	$10.75	$9.65	$9.09	$8.78
11%	$11.37	$10.32	$9.80	$9.52

Tyler has been renting a house for several years. He now has the option to buy the house, but he will need to borrow $120,000. Tyler has spoken to several lending institutions. Each one has offered him loans with different interest rates for different periods of time. Help Tyler compare the different loan options by completing the table below.

Monthly payments on a loan of $120,000

	15 years	20 years	25 years	30 years
7%				
8%				
9%				
10%				
11%				

© 1998 J. Weston Walch, Publisher   *Real-Life Math: Tables, Charts, and Graphs*

12. Class President Election

Goal

To learn about elementary pie and bar graphs in the context of reporting election results.

NCTM Standards Addressed

Standard 2: Mathematics as Communication

Standard 4: Mathematical Connections

Standard 5: Algebra

Standard 6: Functions

Standard 10: Statistics

Teaching Notes

Two graphs are presented side-by-side on the student page. This allows students to compare them critically. These particular graphs use a statistic that has a clear "whole," the population of the class who voted. Other graphs are more comparative.

Context

Bar graphs and pie charts often appear in reports, newspapers, and textbooks. Students need to be able to read them critically and interpret what they say (and don't say). Many software packages also have built-in charts, and students need to know what types of graphs are appropriate in different situations.

Extension Activities

- The newspaper *USA Today* is a wonderful source for graphs and charts.

- Have students search for a graph in a publication they are reading, then write a critique about how readable the graph is and whether another format would have been clearer.

Answers

1. No. No one received a majority of the votes.

2. Yes. Latesha earned a plurality in this election.

3. The runoff would be between Latesha and Touch.

4. Leila got about 18 percent of the vote.

5. Latesha got about as many votes as Bobby and Jane combined.

6. Answers may vary, but most students like the scale included in the bar graph.

7. Answers may vary, but adding a percent statement in each region of the pie chart would make it easier to interpret.

12. Class President Election

The F.W. Parker School recently had an election to choose a class president. After the votes were collected, Mrs. Elman, the principal, counted the votes. She calculated the percentage of votes received by each candidate and then drew graphs of the results. Mrs. Elman chose a horizontal bar graph and a pie chart to show the data. Below are her two graphs. Can you interpret and critique them?

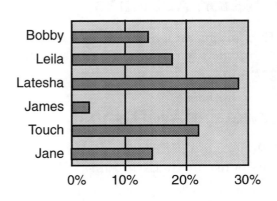

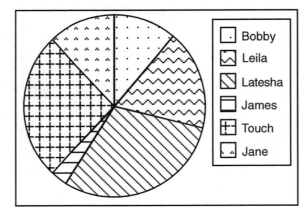

1. In some elections, it is necessary to get 50% of the vote to win. This is called getting a majority. Did any candidate get a majority in this election? If so, who?

    _____

2. If a majority of the vote is not required to win, then a candidate only needs to get the most votes, a plurality, to win. Did any candidate get a plurality in this election? If so, who?

    _____

3. Sometimes, when the winner does not have a majority, a runoff election is held between the top two vote-getters. If this election were run under these rules, who would be in the runoff?

    _____

4. Approximately what percentage of the vote did Leila get?

    _____

5. Latesha got about as many votes as what other two candidates combined?

    _____

6. Which of the two graphs, the bar graph or the pie chart, makes it easier to tell who won? Why?

    _____

7. What would you do to the other graph to make it more informative?

    _____

13. Rating Car Traits

Goal

To learn about augmented bar graphs through reading and interpreting one.

NCTM Standards Addressed

Standard 2: Mathematics as Communication

Standard 4: Mathematical Connections

Standard 5: Algebra

Standard 6: Functions

Standard 10: Statistics

Teaching Notes

Augmented bar graphs can be powerful because they give three kinds of information in only two dimensions. In the graph on this activity sheet, the total number of drivers who rated each category highest is represented by the total height of the bar, but the sections of the bars give you a better sense of what is important to specific age groups.

Context

Augmented bar graphs appear in financial reports and survey results because they add information to the graph but don't necessitate a third dimension.

Extension Activities

Encourage students to find and interpret an augmented bar graph in a newspaper or magazine.

Answers to Worksheet

1. Reputation is the most common response in all age groups.

2. Reputation is the most common response in the 31–50 age group.

3. Reputation is the least common response in the 18–30 age group.

4. Reputation is the most common response in the 51+ age group.

5. About 14% of people aged 31–50 saw appearance as their most important criterion.

6. About 5% of people aged 18–30 saw reputation as their most important criteria.

7. Answers will vary, but the diagonals help with comparing sizes of nonadjacent regions.

13. Rating Car Traits

In a recent survey, drivers from different age groups were asked to identify what they thought was most important in buying a car: appearance, expense, safety, or reputation. One hundred drivers in each of three age groups responded. The results are presented below in an augmented bar graph. Augmented bar graphs present more than one set of data on the same graph. Can you answer the questions below based on the information in the graph?

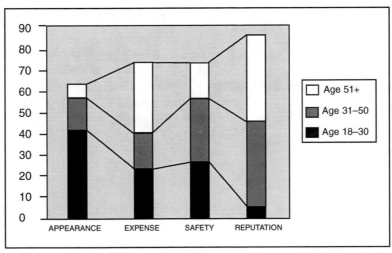

1. Which of the four possible responses is most common among *all* respondents?

_____

2. Which of the responses is most common among people in the 31- to 50-year-old age group? _____

3. Which of the responses is least common among people in the 18- to 30-year-old age group? _____

4. Which of the responses is most common among people in the 51+ year-old age group?

_____

5. What percentage of the 31- to 50-year-old group saw appearance as the most important aspect of choosing a car?

_____

6. What percentage of the 18- to 30-year-old group saw reputation as the most important aspect of choosing a car?

_____

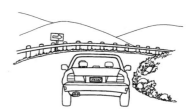

7. What advantages do you see to having the diagonals drawn between the bars in the graph?

_____

14. Reading Stock Graphs

Goal

To practice reading graphs in the setting of a stock price analysis graph.

NCTM Standards Addressed

Standard 2: Mathematics as Communication

Standard 4: Mathematical Connections

Standard 5: Algebra

Standard 6: Functions

Standard 10: Statistics

Teaching Notes

Most students are not familiar with this sort of line graph and will need an explanation of its parts. Each line represents the full range of transaction prices in a given stock entity, and the line out to the right indicates the price of the last trade made that day. This particular graph forms a classic "cup and handle" shape, which many investors believe foretells an increase in stock prices in the short term. Activity 20, Charting Stock Performance, is a good follow-up to this activity.

Context

Stock analysts use a variety of analysis strategies to predict stock and market performance. One common strategy is to create a stock price analysis graph and watch it for trends or patterns that indicate performance.

Extension Activities

Have students follow the stock of their choice for a month and graph its performance daily. When they have enough information, ask them to predict future performance and then monitor their prediction.

Answers

1. September 2—58. September 30th—$56\,^3/_4$. It was down $1\,^1/_4$.

2. The lowest closing price was $56^1/_2$ on Monday, September 23.

3. The high was reached on September 3, October 21, and October 23.

4. On Wednesday, September 25, the stock fluctuated between $56^3/_4$ and $56^7/_8$, a fluctuation of only $^1/_8$ of a dollar per share.

5. The dates that apply are Tuesday, September 3; Tuesday, October 8; Wednesday, October 9; and Thursday, October 17.

6. On Monday, September 9, and Wednesday, September 25, the stock closed at its lowest price for the day.

7. In the week of October 7 the price went from $57^3/_8$ to $58^1/_4$ for the largest one-week change in closing prices.

14. Reading Stock Graphs

Sarah Twombly takes her job as a stock analyst seriously. She follows the performance of individual stocks on a day-to-day basis by creating a stock price analysis graph. Sarah uses this graph to watch for trends or patterns that predict how the stock will perform. At the end of each business day, she makes a line on the graph. The top end of the line marks the highest price paid for the stock that day. The bottom end of the line marks the lowest price. She also places a tick mark out to the right at the price at which the stock last traded that afternoon (*the closing price*). On the graph below, on September 10, Camzo sold for a high of $58\frac{1}{2}$, and a low of 58. Its closing price that day was $58\frac{1}{8}$.

Here is Sarah's graph for an eight-week period of the performance of Camzo, Inc. She needs to get information from this graph for a report she is writing. Can you help?

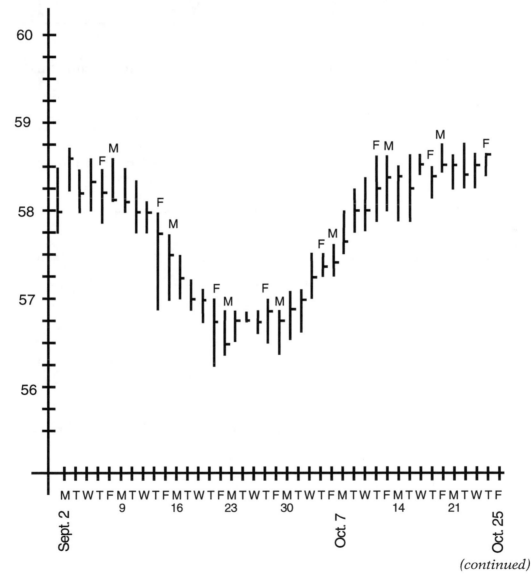

(continued)

14. **Reading Stock Graphs** (continued)

1. Sarah needs to report on the change in the price of Camzo stock in the month of September. What was the closing price of the stock on September 2? What was the closing price of the stock on September 30? What change had there been?

   _____

   _____

   _____

2. What was the lowest closing price for the stock on any day represented by this graph?

   _____

3. The stock sold for its highest price of $58\frac{3}{4}$ on three days during the time this graph covers. What were they?

   _____

4. Which day showed the least fluctuation in the stock's price? How much did it fluctuate on that day?

   _____

5. Name a day on the graph when the stock never sold for as little as the previous day's closing price.

   _____

6. Name a day when the stock closed at its lowest price for the day.

   _____

7. During which week did the price change the most between Monday's close and Friday's close?

   _____

15. Hard Disk Drive Performance

Goal

To practice reading graphs in the context of evaluating technological equipment.

NCTM Standards Addressed

Standard 2: Mathematics as Communication

Standard 4: Mathematical Connections

Standard 5: Algebra

Standard 6: Functions

Standard 10: Statistics

Teaching Notes

The software that generates these graphs is highly specialized. Created by Digital Processing Systems, Inc., it evaluates the speed, in megabytes per second, at which the disk reader can read information as the reader moves out to the outer edge of the disk. The location is the percent of the distance from the inner edge of writeable space to the outer edge of readable space traveled by the reader. The number of sample points determines the speed of the test and the accuracy of the graph.

Context

Computer disk drives, disks, and readers carry immense amounts of information. The speed with which the information is read determines whether it is possible to complete certain types of projects. A videographer, for instance, has whole series of pictures, each of which requires large amounts of information space. They must be read at a certain speed or the images get distorted.

Extension Activities

Computer technology changes so rapidly that even experts can get confused by the all the variations on concepts. A local programmer might come in to talk with students about how calculation speed and reading speed affect most people's activities. Some of your students may know enough about this to do a presentation.

Answers

1. (1a) The title of the x-axis is "Relative Location (%)." (1b) The x-axis is the percentage of the radius of the disk that the reader has moved from the inside edge to the outside edge.

2. (2a) The title of the y-axis is "MB/SEC." (2b) The y-axis is megabytes per second that the reader is reading successfully.

3. Cole evaluated a Microp-3243-191128RFA and a Seagate-ST19171N drive.

4. None of the Microp drive and about $72\frac{1}{2}\%$ of the Seagate drive.

5. The Seagate drive is more effective for Cole's purposes.

6. The software is evaluating the drive at 64 different points on its surface.

Name _____ Date _____

15. Hard Disk Drive Performance

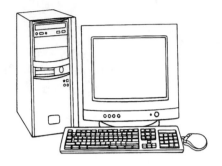

Cole Tamminen, a videographer, uses a video camera to film motion pictures. He downloads the images onto his computer, storing them electronically on the hard disk drive. Cole edits his films on the computer, utilizing a hard disk reader when working with the electronic images. The hard disk reader compensates for information stored at different locations on the disk. The location is the percentage of the distance from the inner edge to the outer edge of writeable space. Information stored toward the outer edge of a $5\frac{1}{2}$-inch disk spins past the reader much faster than information stored at the inner edge. Cole's images would be distorted without a hard disk reader to adjust them to the proper speed. Cole has an analyzer that evaluates whether his various hard disk readers are working properly. The analyzer produced performance graphs for two of Cole's hard drives. Can you analyze them?

1. a. What is the title of the *x*-axis? _____

   b. What does this title mean? _____

2. a. What is the title of the *y*-axis? _____

   b. What does this title mean? _____

3. What types of drives or "devices" has Cole evaluated?

   _____

4. Cole needs the reader to be able to interpret at least 9.000 megabytes per second. According to these graphs, what percentage of each drive can attain this speed?

   _____

5. Which of the two drives is more effective for Cole's work?

   _____

6. The graphs indicate that there are "64 sample points." What do you suppose this means?

   _____

(continued)

15. Hard Disk Drive Performance *(continued)*

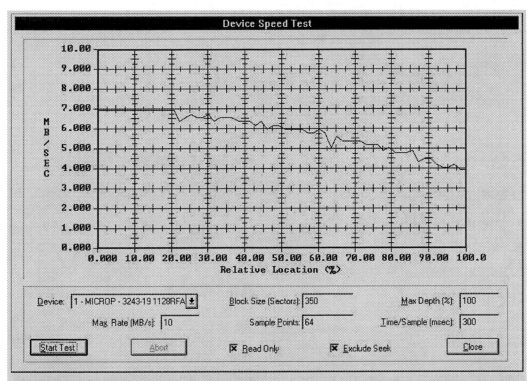

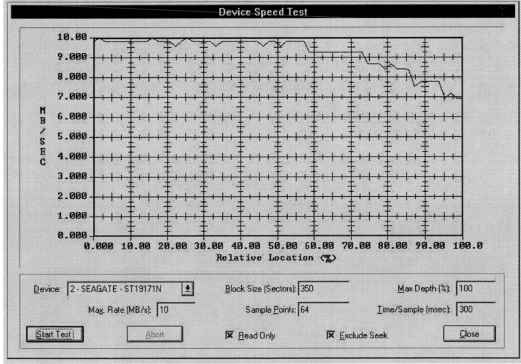

Device Speed Test graphs are copyrighted by Digital Processing Systems, Inc. and are used with permission.

16. Grading on a Curve

Goal

To learn about stem-and-leaf plots in the context of analyzing exam scores.

NCTM Standards Addressed

Standard 2: Mathematics as Communication

Standard 4: Mathematical Connections

Standard 5: Algebra

Standard 6: Functions

Standard 10: Statistics

Teaching Notes

The advantage of a stem-and-leaf plot is the quick-reference visual analysis it provides. This stem and leaf does not have all data in order, so students must be careful in calculating the median. The median score is the middle score when the scores are in ascending or descending order. The mean score is the sum of the scores divided by the number of scores.

Context

Students often ask, "Are you going to grade this on a curve?" Showing them an exercise that demonstrates how you would configure data to "grade on a curve" often convinces students that they don't want their tests graded this way!

Extension Activities

Stem-and-leaf plots are visual and informative. Have students collect data on heart rates or some other numerical result and ask them to create a stem-and-leaf plot.

Answers

1. The three scores that were earned by more than one student were 100, 77, and 68.

2. The three highest scores on the test were 100, 100, and 97.

3. The three lowest scores on the test were 56, 57, and 59.

4. The median score on the test was 77.

5. The mean score was 78.3, so this was a good test by Betsy's standards.

6. Although not exact, this data set approximates a normal distribution.

Name _____   Date _____

16. Grading on a Curve

Persis Lynn is a teacher. She recently gave a test and decided to arrange the scores in a stem-and-leaf plot so that she would see how they were distributed. A stem is the first digit(s) of a number; the stems are listed in numerical order to create categories. A leaf is the ones digit of a number; the leaves are listed beside their stems, or first digits. The stem-and-leaf plot allows Persis to see if the test scores fit the "normal" or "bell" curve that is commonly used in grading exams. Persis also wants to know the mean and median of the test scores. The mean is determined by dividing the sum of all the test scores by the number of scores. The median is the center number when the test scores are placed in order numerically. The mode is the number that appears most frequently in the set of data. See if you can help Persis interpret the graph of her test data.

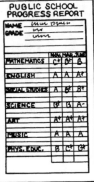

10 | 0 0

9 | 3 7 2 1

8 | 2 7 6 1 5

7 | 3 7 7 6 5 4 1

6 | 9 4 8 8

5 | 7 6 9

1. Which scores were earned by more than one student?

_____

2. What were the three highest scores that students earned on this test?

_____

3. What were the three lowest scores that students earned on this test?

_____

4. What was the median score on this test? _____

5. Persis believes that she has given a good test if the mean score is between 72 and 81. Is this a good test by her standards?

_____

6. If the scores of a test are normally distributed, their frequency table should look something like this:

   Does Persis Lynn's data set look like a normal distribution to you? _____

17. Baseball Attendance

Goal

To learn about scatter-plot graphs in the context of evaluating baseball attendance statistics.

NCTM Standards Addressed

Standard 1: Mathematics as Problem Solving

Standard 2: Mathematics as Communication

Standard 4: Mathematical Connections

Standard 5: Algebra

Standard 6: Functions

Standard 10: Statistics

Teaching Notes

Once the students have chosen their scales and how they wish to indicate their data, scatter-plot graphing is just plotting points. Evaluating this graph is difficult because of the size of Los Angeles's population. Students might try focusing the graph on all the other teams to try and find a pattern.

Context

Much is made of the "size of the market" in determining a baseball team's competitiveness and profitability. Comparing populations and attendance does not consider revenues from TV rights or team paraphernalia, but it is interesting to note that there does not seem to be a clear correlation in this graph between smaller populations and smaller crowds.

Extension Activities

Ask students to consider other factors in analyzing this graph. A great deal of business understanding can be gained from considering the arguments on both sides.

ANSWERS

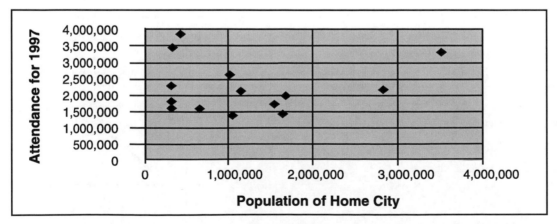

Since the two highest attendance figures are for teams in relatively small cities, population does not appear to be a major factor in major league attendance.

17. Baseball Attendance

There has been a lot of talk in the media recently about large- and small-market teams and how they can compete. Alfred Frawley was curious to see if there really was a connection between the listed population of the hometown for a given team and that team's success at the box office. He has collected information on 1997 attendance at all National League baseball games and the population of their home cities. Although some of the cities have much larger metropolitan areas than others, Alfred stuck to the population of the cities themselves. Alfred would now like to make a scatter-plot graph of the results to see if he can find any patterns in the data. Can you help create the graph and give your interpretation?

Team	Population of Home City	1997 Home Attendance
Atlanta Braves	394,017	3,463,988
Chicago Cubs	2,783,726	2,190,308
Cincinnati Reds	364,040	1,785,788
Colorado Rockies	467,610	3,888,453
Florida Marlins	358,548	2,364,387
Houston Astros	1,630,553	2,046,811
Los Angeles Dodgers	3,485,398	3,318,886
Montreal Expos	1,015,420	1,497,609
New York Mets	1,487,536	1,766,174
Philadelphia Phillies	1,585,577	1,490,638
Pittsburgh Pirates	369,879	1,657,022
San Diego Padres	1,110,549	2,089,336
San Francisco Giants	723,959	1,690,831
St. Louis Cardinals	993,529	2,658,357

(continued)

17. Baseball Attendance (continued)

Start by finding the range of the data so that you can choose a scale for the graph. Then decide what information you will put on the *x* axis and on the *y* axis. Finally, use the data in the table on the preceding page to plot the graph.

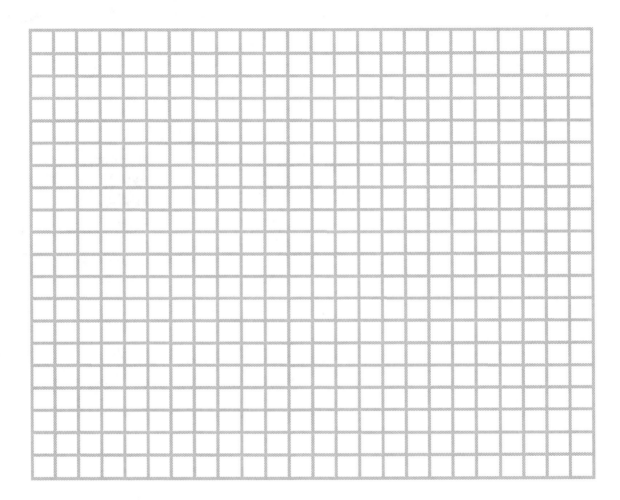

Based on this graph, do you think there is a correlation between hometown population and attendance at games?

_____

18. Average Rental Prices

Goal

To learn about box-and-whisker plots as a method for statistical analysis.

NCTM Standards Addressed

Standard 1: Mathematics as Problem Solving

Standard 2: Mathematics as Communication

Standard 4: Mathematical Connections

Standard 5: Algebra

Standard 6: Functions

Standard 10: Statistics

Teaching Notes

To form a box-and-whisker plot put all of your data in order from least to greatest. Determine the median (middle number or mean of two middle numbers). Separate the data into two lists at the median and deter-mine the median of each list. These two medians are known as the "hinges" of the graph. Draw a rectangular box to depict the distance between the two hinges, with a line at the original median. Draw two lines or "whiskers" out from the ends of the box to the maximum and minimum values of the data. The quartiles are found in the right whisker, the right end of the box, the left end of the box, and the left whisker.

Context

Statisticians use box-and-whisker plots to determine the compactness of data. Many governmental statisticians collect and analyze data on costs of living in given areas this way.

Extension Activities

Have students discover other types of data that could be represented in a box-and-whisker format.

Answers

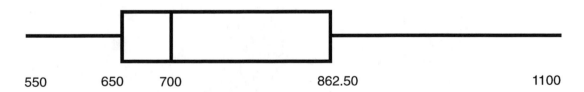

| 550 | 650 | 700 | 862.50 | 1100 |

Ross can expect to find an apartment in the $650 to $700 range.

18. Average Rental Prices

Ross Blair is moving to Chicago. He is trying to figure out how much he will need to pay for housing. He canvassed his new coworkers to learn what they pay for rent. He has decided to create a box-and-whisker graph of the results to analyze his probable costs. To do this, Ross will place all the data in order from least to greatest to determine the median (middle number or mean of two middle numbers). He will then separate the data into two lists at this median and determine the median of each new list. These two medians are known as the "hinges" of the graph. Ross will draw a number line, with the lowest rent at one end of the line and the highest rent at the other end. He will add a rectangular box between the two hinges, or sedcondary median. The parts of the number line that are not included in the box—called "whiskers"—show the high and low rent ranges. The white plot is then divided into quartiles. The right whisker is the first quartile, the right-hand section of the box is the second quartile, the left hand section is the third quartile, and the left whisker is the fourth quartile.

Use the rental data below to create a box-and-whisker plot.

$580	$1,025	$950	$650	$700
$675	$700	$850	$725	$1,100
$715	$700	$775	$625	$700
$650	$875	$550	$895	$775
$725	$650	$675	$575	$875

What range of prices should Ross expect if he plans to find an apartment in the third quartile of the price range?

© 1998 J. Weston Walch, Publisher   *Real-Life Math: Tables, Charts, and Graphs*

19. The "Juiced" Ball Argument

Goal

To learn about drawing broken-line graphs using two variables from baseball statistics.

NCTM Standards Addressed

Standard 1: Mathematics as Problem Solving

Standard 2: Mathematics as Communication

Standard 4: Mathematical Connections

Standard 5: Algebra

Standard 6: Functions

Standard 10: Statistics

Teaching Notes

Drawing a broken-line graph is a matter of setting up your axes, plotting your points, and connecting them in a reasonable order. Using time as one variable gives an easy order to this graphing project.

Context

Baseball statisticians often use home-run totals as a way of identifying changes in the size of the league or the construction of a baseball. By graphing home run results over time, it is possible to observe trends rather than short-term fluctuations.

Extension Activities

These data also lend themselves to constructing a bar graph.

Answers

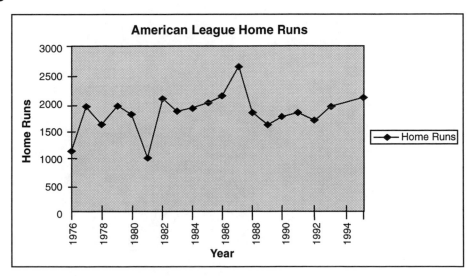

The trend appears to be flat but expansion in 1998 will likely cause another upswing, if the graph was extended to the present day.

19. The "Juiced" Ball Argument

Henry Cohn works for Stats, Inc.™ in Skokie, IL. His job is to follow statistical trends in baseball and make projections from this information. Henry has been asked to make a graph of the number of home runs hit in the American League since 1975 and then project what will happen in the next couple of years. He has gathered the following data. Can you help him prepare a line graph and make his projections?

Home runs hit in American League: 1976 – 1995

Year	Home runs
1976	1,122
1977	2,013
1978	1,680
1979	2,006
1980	1,844
1981	1,062
1982	2,080
1983	1,903
1984	1,980
1985	2,178

Year	Home runs
1986	2,290
1987	2,634
1988	1,901
1989	1,718
1990	1,796
1991	1,953
1992	1,776
1993	2,074
1994	1,774
1995	2,164

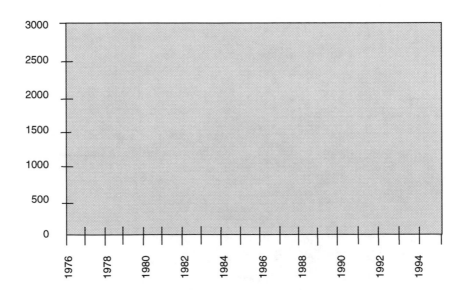

What trend would you advise Henry to predict? _____

20. Charting Stock Performance

Goal

To learn about graphing through drawing an augmented line graph of a stock's price over time.

NCTM Standards Addressed

Standard 1: Mathematics as Problem Solving

Standard 2: Mathematics as Communication

Standard 4: Mathematical Connections

Standard 5: Algebra

Standard 6: Functions

Standard 10: Statistics

Teaching Notes

It is important to connect the high and low marks for the day, and then draw the tail at the closing price. This activity works well with Activity 14, Reading Stock Graphs.

Context

Stock analysts use this type of graph to follow individual stocks and the market as a whole. Graphs of this type appear in the *Wall Street Journal* daily.

Extension Activities

Have students pick a stock and follow it for a month or so, graphing its progress.

Answers

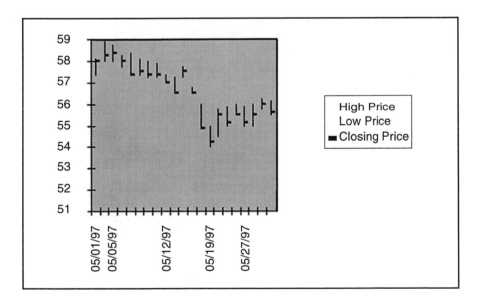

(Answers will vary.) Future doesn't look too promising because of the steady and gradual decrease in price over the past month. Wouldn't recommend.

20. Charting Stock Performance

Kaley Trafton is charting the performance of her stock in Norbell & Co. She isn't able to keep up with her graphing, so she has her daughter jot down the high, low, and closing prices of the stock each day and then store it in a spreadsheet for her. Each month Kaley sits down and draws the graph of the stock's performance to see how things are going. Kaley indicates each day's range of high and low prices by drawing a vertical line between them. She draws a small horizontal tick mark on the vertical line to show the closing price of the stock each day.

Using the table below, draw a graph of the stock's performance and make some projections based on it. (Since the stock market is not open on weekends and holidays, the only days on the chart are weekdays when the stock actually traded.)

Date	High Price	Low Price	Closing Price
05/01/97	58 1/8	57 3/8	58
05/02/97	58 7/8	58	58 1/4
05/05/97	58 3/4	58	58 3/8
05/06/97	58 1/4	57 3/4	58
05/07/97	58 3/8	57 3/8	57 3/8
05/08/97	58 1/8	57 3/8	57 1/2
05/09/97	58	57 1/4	57 3/8
05/12/97	57 7/8	57 1/4	57 3/8
05/13/97	57 3/8	57	57
05/14/97	57 1/4	56 1/2	56 1/2
05/15/97	57 3/4	57 1/4	57 1/2
05/16/97	56 3/4	56 1/2	56 1/2
05/19/97	56	54 7/8	54 7/8
05/20/97	55	54	54 1/4
05/21/97	55 3/4	54 1/2	55 1/2
05/22/97	55 7/8	55	55 1/8
05/23/97	56	55 1/2	55 1/2
05/27/97	55 7/8	55	55 1/8
05/28/97	56	55	55 1/2
05/29/97	56 1/4	55 3/4	56
05/30/97	56 1/8	55 1/2	55 5/8

(continued)

20. **Charting Stock Performance** *(continued)*

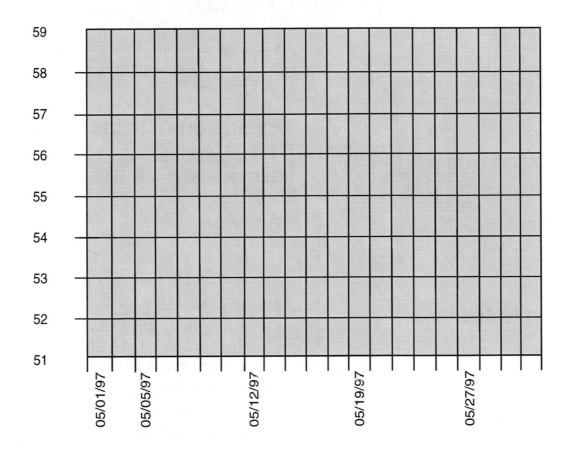

If you were making recommendations to Kaley about this stock and its future, based solely on this graph, what would you recommend and why?

_____

_____

_____

21. Genealogy

Goal

To learn how to read charts in the context of genealogy research and a family tree.

NCTM Standards Addressed

Standard 2: Mathematics as Communication

Standard 4: Mathematical Connections

Standard 5: Algebra

Standard 10: Statistics

Teaching Notes

A well-researched family tree is easy to follow, but it is a bit harder to understand the difference between "first cousin, once-removed," and "second cousin." You may want to clarify this concept for yourself in order to answer students' questions accurately.

Context

Many people are fascinated by their family history. Most Americans trace back their history a few generations and then get lost in the emigration of a relative from a far-off place. Researching family histories is both a business and a hobby for some.

Extension Activities

Ask students to interview their parents or grandparents to create their own family tree.

Answers

1. Erin and Jim have four children.

2. Susan Boyle married David Kelty.

3. Susan Smith's grandfather is Jim Bull.

4. The twins in the family are Arthur and Susan Smith, Megan and Bethany Coomer, and Barbara and Mary Bull.

5. Erin Bull is Pam Kelty-Coomer's niece. Pam is Erin's aunt.

6. Bethany and Arthur are second cousins.

7. Megan is Karen's great-granddaughter. Karen is Megan's great-grandmother.

8. Katharine and Jim are first cousins, once-removed.

9. Orchid is Richard's grandniece. Richard is Orchid's great-uncle.

21. Genealogy

Jo Wallace is an avid collector of details about her family tree and others'. She researches people's genealogies to help them see how they are related to other family members. Jo explains that a family member who is the child of your first cousin, is your "first cousin, once-removed" (related at the level of first cousins, but offset one generation). However, a family member who is the child of your mother's first cousin is your "second cousin" (same generation, children of cousins). Below are some questions about a family tree Jo has researched for a client. The family tree is shown on the next page. See if you can answer the questions about it.

1. How many children did Erin Kelty and Jim Bull have? _____

2. Whom did Susan Boyle marry? _____

3. What is the name of Susan Smith's grandfather? _____

   _____

4. There are three sets of twins in this family tree. Name at least two of them.

   _____

   _____

5. What is the relationship between Erin Bull and Pam Kelty-Coomer?

   _____

6. What is the relationship between Bethany Coomer and Arthur Smith?

   _____

7. What is the relationship between Megan Coomer and Karen Douglass Kelty?

   _____

8. What is the relationship between Katharine Coomer and Jim Kelty?

   _____

9. What is the relationship between Orchid Boone and Richard Kelty?

   _____

(continued)

21. Genealogy *(continued)*

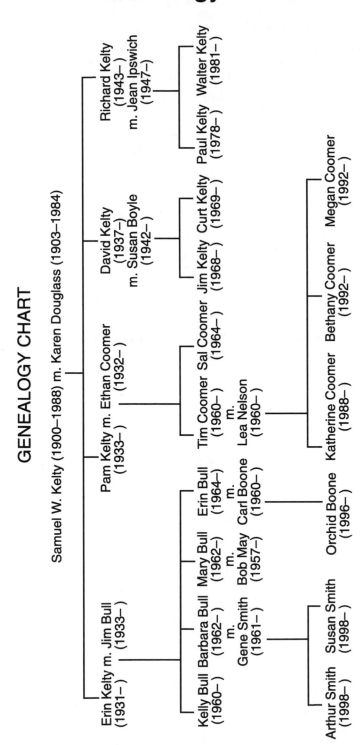

GENEALOGY CHART

Samuel W. Kelty (1900–1988) m. Karen Douglass (1903–1984)

Erin Kelty m. Jim Bull (1933–)

Kelly Bull (1960–)

Barbara Bull (1962–)
m.
Gene Smith (1961–)

Arthur Smith (1998–)

Susan Smith (1998–)

Mary Bull (1962–)
m.
Bob May (1957–)

Erin Bull (1964–)
m.
Carl Boone (1960–)

Orchid Boone (1996–)

Pam Kelty m. Ethan Coomer (1932–)

Tim Coomer (1960–)

Sal Coomer (1964–)
m.
Lea Nelson (1960–)

Katherine Coomer (1988–)

Bethany Coomer (1992–)

Megan Coomer (1992–)

David Kelty (1937–)
m. Susan Boyle (1942–)

Jim Kelty (1968–)

Curt Kelty (1969–)

Richard Kelty (1943–)
m. Jean Ipswich (1947–)

Paul Kelty (1978–)

Walter Kelty (1981–)

Erin Kelty (1931–)

54   *Real-Life Math: Tables, Charts, and Graphs*

22. Reading Work Schedules

Goal

To practice reading charts with a weekly work schedule that might be found in a restaurant or other workplace.

NCTM Standards Addressed

Standard 2: Mathematics as Communication

Standard 4: Mathematical Connections

Standard 5: Algebra

Standard 10: Statistics

Teaching Notes

This worksheet is very straightforward. You might want to ask students to double-check that Andy has the right number of workers on at each time of day. A different table could be used to double-check Andy's work. This activity works well with Activity 26, Making Work Schedules.

Context

Many people have hourly jobs with changeable schedules. Learning how to read such a schedule and interpret it is an important part of being at work on time.

Extension Activities

If your students work, you might ask them to bring in copies of the schedules used in their workplaces.

Answers

1. Ling is scheduled to work 39 hours this week.

2. Yes, Bishop will work 27.5 hours this week.

3. Yes, Chris is off Monday, Wednesday, and Friday.

4. The closing managers are Ling (M–W, F–Sa), Sansón and Corinna (Th), and Bishop (Su).

5. The opening managers are Hoyt (M–W, F), Chris (Th), Bishop (Sa), and Peyo (Su).

6. Peyo is doubling back, working Tuesday night and Wednesday morning.

Name _____   Date _____

22. Reading Work Schedules

Andy runs a bakery/restaurant in Chicago. Each week he schedules his "front staff" to cover the three morning shifts, five midday shifts, and two evening shifts for Monday through Friday. (On weekends, fewer work.) Because he hires a number of part-time workers, the schedule changes weekly. Each week Andy asks his employees if they have any special schedule requests. Then every Friday morning, Andy posts the schedule for the following Monday through Sunday on the bulletin board, so that everyone will know when they are working. Below is last week's schedule. Can you answer the questions about it on the next page?

EMPLOYEE	MON.	TUES.	WED.	THURS.	FRI.	SAT.	SUN.
LING	12 P.M.–8 P.M.	12 P.M.–8 P.M.	12 P.M.–8 P.M.		12 P.M.–8 P.M.	10 A.M.–5 P.M.	
HOYT	6:30 A.M.–1:30 P.M.	6:30 A.M.–1:30 P.M.	6:30 A.M.–1:30 P.M.		6:30 A.M.–1:30 P.M.		
VINCE	7 A.M.–1 P.M.		7 A.M.–1 P.M.	7 A.M.–1 P.M.			
CHRIS V.		7 A.M.–1 P.M.		6:30 A.M.–1:30 P.M.		10 A.M.–4 P.M.	11 A.M.–4 P.M.
CORINNA	11 A.M.–7 P.M.	10 A.M.–4 P.M.	10 A.M.–4 P.M.	12 P.M.–8 P.M.	2 P.M.–7 P.M.		
SANSON		11:30 A.M.–1:30 P.M.		12 P.M.–8 P.M.	2 P.M.–1:30 P.M.		
BISHOP	7:30 A.M.–1 P.M.		4 P.M.–7 P.M.		7 A.M.–1 P.M.	6:30 A.M.–1:30– P.M.	11 A.M.–5 P.M.
PEYO		4 P.M.–7 P.M.	7:30 A.M.–1 P.M.			7 A.M.–1 P.M.	6:30 A.M.–1:30 P.M.
ANDY		7:30 A.M.–9:30 A.M.		7:30 A.M.–1 P.M.	7:30 A.M.–1 P.M.		7 A.M.–1 P.M.

(continued)

Name _____   Date _____

22. Reading Work Schedules *(continued)*

1. How many hours will Ling work next week?

   _____

2. Bishop worked only 20 hours a week for the last few weeks. He asked Andy to give him more hours now that his final exams are over. Was Andy able to accommodate Bishop's wishes?

3. Chris Van Buren is taking classes on Mondays, Wednesdays, and Fridays and has asked not to work on class days if at all possible. Was Andy able to accommodate Chris?

   _____

4. The closing manager is always scheduled to work an hour past closing time (7:00 P.M. weekdays, 4:00 P.M. weekends) so they can cash out. Who are the closing managers this week?

   _____

5. The opening manager is always scheduled to work a half hour before opening time (7:00 A.M.) so they can open up. Who are the opening managers this week?

   _____

6. When an employee works a closing shift one day and an opening shift the next, it is called "doubling back." Andy usually asks employees if they are willing to double back. Is anyone scheduled to double back this week?

   _____

23. The Marker Game

Goal

To use rows and columns to identify places in a grid, and to think about the relationships between consecutive squares in that grid.

NCTM Standards Addressed

Standard 1: Mathematics as Problem Solving

Standard 2: Mathematics as Communication

Standard 3: Mathematics as Reasoning

Standard 4: Mathematical Connections

Standard 5: Algebra

Standard 10: Statistics

Teaching Notes

This game is a great hands-on learning activity. You can clear a space in the room, make a masking tape grid on the floor, and get students moving. The last two questions on the worksheet are intentionally open-ended, and the answers are based on experience, not on mathematical proof.

Context

There is no real-life context for this game, but it raises a number of good theoretical questions in the context of grids and charts.

Extension Activities

- Students can create diagrams in which they use a certain number of markers.

- The game of Battleship™ makes good use of a grid, as does a shareware software game called Minesweeper v.3™.

Answers

	A	B	C	D	E	F	G	H
1	1	1	2	●	2	1	1	0
2	1	●	2	1	2	●	2	1
3	2	2	1	0	1	2	3	●
4	●	1	1	1	1	1	●	2
5	1	1	1	●	1	1	1	1
6	0	1	2	2	1	1	1	1
7	1	2	●	1	0	1	●	1
8	●	2	1	1	0	1	1	1

1. There are two markers in F3, placed by the students in F2 and G4.

2. There are no markers in E7. It is not adjacent to any students.

3. The largest number of markers possible in one square is eight. Eight students would have to form a square around that square to get eight markers into it.

4. Hibah would have used five markers and kept three if he was in an edge space that was not a corner, and had no neighbor squares occupied by his classmates. Squares A4 and D1 fit these criteria.

5. The greatest number of markers it is possible to use is 78. The following grid is one way of reaching 78 used markers:

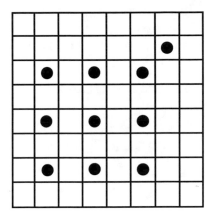

6. The smallest number of markers it is possible to use is 16. The following grid is one way of reaching 16 used markers:

Name _____ Date _____

23. The Marker Game

A grid is painted on the floor of a large room. There are eight rows and eight columns in the grid. Ten students are asked to enter the room and stand in one square of the grid. Each student has eight markers. They are asked to place a marker in each square of the grid that is next to their square, horizontally, vertically, and diagonally. Students may not place a marker in a square occupied by another student and may not place a marker outside the grid. They may put a marker in a square that already contains a marker.

In the game grid below, students are identified by black dots. See if you can identify how many markers belong in each square *and* answer some further questions.

	A	B	C	D	E	F	G	H
1				●				
2		●				●		
3								●
4	●						●	
5				●				
6								
7			●				●	
8	●							

(continued)

23. The Marker Game *(continued)*

1. How many markers lie in square F3? _____

2. How many markers lie in square E7? _____

3. What is the largest number of markers that could be in one square? How could this happen?

   _____

4. Hibah left the room with three markers in his pocket. He said he had put out all the markers he was supposed to use and that no one had been standing next to him in any direction. Identify which squares Hibah might have stood on.

   _____

5. A teacher asked his students to arrange themselves in such a way that they would use up as many of their markers as possible. What configuration would you suggest?

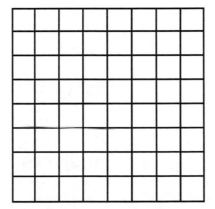

6. A teacher asked her students to try to arrange themselves in such a way that they would use up as few of their markers as possible. What configuration would you suggest?

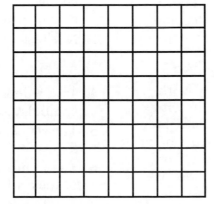

24. Reading PERT Charts

Goal

To learn about reading charts in the context of PERT charts.

NCTM Standards Addressed

Standard 2: Mathematics as Communication

Standard 4: Mathematical Connections

Standard 5: Algebra

Standard 6: Functions

Standard 10: Statistics

Standard 12: Discrete Mathematics

Teaching Notes

The PERT (periodic evaluation and review technique) chart was created during the building of the Polaris submarine. The chart allows you to see which tasks in a multitask project are "critical" (must be completed on time in order for other projects to be completed on time). The tasks are indicated on the chart by lines. Each task that depends on other tasks has a line drawn from its left end to those tasks' right end. Redundant links are erased (task 6 depends on tasks 3 and 4, but task 4 is already dependent on task 3, so it is "redundant" to say that task 6 depends on task 3). The job completion time is then projected by working backward. Starting at the far right with 0, you add the time needed to complete the last task. That number is then carried along the prerequisite links to previous tasks, and then their lengths are added. When one task has two or more tasks attached to its right end, the largest number coming from those tasks is added. The "critical path" is the collection of tasks that actually contributed their lengths to the completion time. This activity works well with Activity 27, Creating PERT charts.

Context

PERT charts are great for multitask projects. Building a car, like most manufacturing projects, is a complicated process, and the table has been simplified significantly for this worksheet. This technique has been effective for some enormous projects and is still used by government agencies and construction supervisors.

Extension Activities

See extension notes for Activity 27.

Answers

1. Task 1 (chassis and engine) and task 5 (seats and interior) require the most time.
2. Yes. Tasks 6 and 7 could be interchanged because they are independent of each other.
3. No. Tasks 3 and 4 could not be interchanged because task 4 depends on task 3.
4. Task 5 depends on task 1 (chassis and engine) and task 4 (steering controls).
5. The critical path is through tasks 1, 3, 4, 5, 6, and 8.
6. The minimum amount of time (length of the critical path) is $13\frac{1}{2}$ hours.
7. No. Tires are not part of the critical path, so more time can be used.

24. Reading PERT Charts

Building cars is a tricky business. Not only are there a number of parts that need to be put on, but the timing needs to be right so that one department isn't standing around waiting for another department. Below is a table of the departments that need to work on a car and the time they need to complete their jobs. Below that is a PERT (periodic evaluation and review technique) chart of the construction of a car. A PERT chart is a visual way of showing the steps in a process. First, you decide what all the steps are, and list each step. Next you work out how long, on average, it takes to complete each step. On the PERT chart, each step is shown as a thin horizontal line, with a circle at each end. The chart moves from left to right. The first task is shown at the left of the chart, with the time it takes to complete, and is labeled "1." The next step is labeled "2," and so on. See if you can interpret the table and chart in order to answer the following questions about building a car.

If a step cannot be started until another step has been finished, a heavy line is drawn frm the right-hand circle of the earlier step to the left-hand circle of the later step. For example, if you made a PERT chart for mailing a letter, the step "sealing the envelope" could only be done if the step "inserting the letter" had already by completed. The chart would connect these two steps by a line. However, the step "putting on the stamp" could be done either before or after the other two steps, so it would not be connected to either of them.

The time it takes to complete a project can be found by adding up times, from the last step at the right of the chart to the first step at the left. When one task has two or more tasks attached to its right end, the largest number coming from those tasks is added. The tasks whose times make up the completion time form the "critical path" for the project.

Department	Prerequisite Tasks	Hours Needed
1. Chassis & Engine	————	5
2. Fuel System	1	1
3. Wheels	1	$\frac{1}{2}$
4. Steering Controls	1, 3	2
5. Seats & Interior	1, 4	3
6. Doors	1, 2, 4, 5	1
7. Tires	1, 3	$\frac{1}{2}$
8. Glass	1, 4, 5, 6	2

(continued)

24. Reading PERT Charts *(continued)*

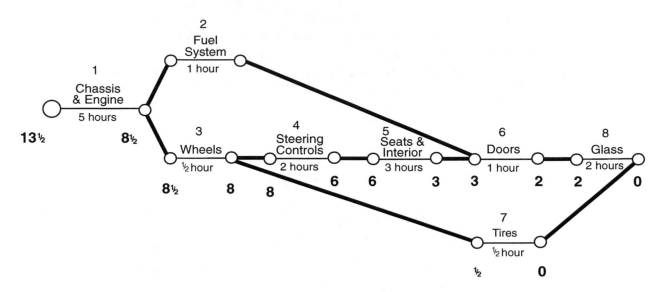

1. Which two tasks require the most time to complete?

   _____

2. Could the tires be done as task 6 and the doors as task 7?

   _____

3. Could the steering controls be done as task 3 and the wheels as task 4?

   _____

4. What tasks must be completed before "5. Seats & Interior"?

   _____

5. What is the critical path on the process of making a car?

   _____

6. What is the minimum amount of time in which a car can be completed?

   _____

7. If a piece of machinery broke and it took one hour extra to finish
   the tire installation, would the minimum amount of time to build
   the car change? Why? _____

   _____

25. The Electoral College

Goal

To learn about creating charts using results from the 1996 presidential election.

NCTM Standards Addressed

Standard 1: Mathematics as Problem Solving

Standard 2: Mathematics as Communication

Standard 4: Mathematical Connections

Standard 5: Algebra

Standard 10: Statistics

Teaching Notes

Charts that represent statistics and use area rather than numbers can be misleading. In creating this chart, students will find that the election looks closer than it was because some large states with small populations voted for Mr. Dole, the loser of the election.

Context

Charts of election results can be found in atlases and encyclopedias. They are helpful in identifying areas of the country voting in blocs, but because electoral college votes are distributed based on population, not on area, these graphics do not accurately represent results.

Extension Activities

Ask students to create a more informative graph by changing the size of the states to represent the number of electoral votes of each state. Texas, California, and New York become quite large!

Answers

Answers will vary. Most students will color the map with two different colors. Some will write in state names and electoral votes on the map. Others will add keys and information off to the side.

25. The Electoral College

Nathan Lammi is a political researcher for a reference text company. He is responsible for generating the information that will be turned into graphics, charts, and tables accompanying an article about presidential elections. Nathan has been asked to produce a table and accompanying map of the results of the 1996 election. He has created the table below, but he needs some help with his map. Can you help create the map chart to go with the table on the map on the following page?

State	Votes	Winner	State	Votes	Winner
Alabama	9	Dole	Montana	3	Dole
Alaska	3	Dole	Nebraska	5	Dole
Arizona	8	Clinton	Nevada	4	Clinton
Arkansas	6	Clinton	New Hampshire	4	Clinton
California	54	Clinton	New Jersey	15	Clinton
Colorado	8	Dole	New Mexico	5	Clinton
Connecticut	8	Clinton	New York	33	Clinton
Delaware	3	Clinton	North Carolina	14	Dole
Dist. of Col.	3	Clinton	North Dakota	3	Dole
Florida	25	Clinton	Ohio	21	Clinton
Georgia	13	Dole	Oklahoma	8	Dole
Hawaii	4	Clinton	Oregon	7	Clinton
Idaho	4	Dole	Pennsylvania	23	Clinton
Illinois	22	Clinton	Rhode Island	4	Clinton
Indiana	12	Dole	South Carolina	8	Dole
Iowa	7	Clinton	South Dakota	3	Dole
Kansas	6	Dole	Tennessee	11	Clinton
Kentucky	8	Clinton	Texas	32	Dole
Louisiana	9	Clinton	Utah	5	Dole
Maine	4	Clinton	Vermont	3	Clinton
Maryland	10	Clinton	Virginia	13	Dole
Massachusetts	12	Clinton	Washington	11	Clinton
Michigan	18	Clinton	West Virginia	5	Clinton
Minnesota	10	Clinton	Wisconsin	11	Clinton
Mississippi	7	Dole	Wyoming	3	Dole
Missouri	11	Clinton			

(continued)

Name _____   Date _____

25. The Electoral College *(continued)*

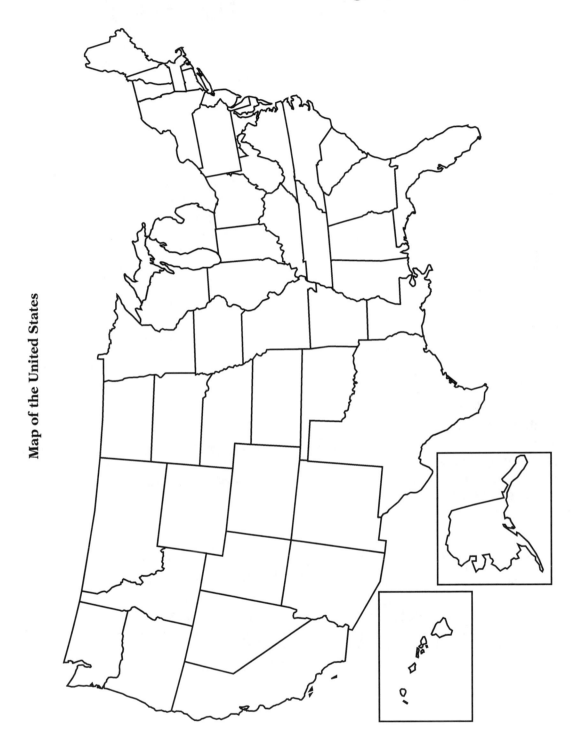

Map of the United States

26. Making Work Schedules

Goal

To create a chart representing a weekly work schedule that might be found in a restaurant or other workplace.

NCTM Standards Addressed

Standard 1: Mathematics as Problem Solving

Standard 2: Mathematics as Communication

Standard 3: Mathematics as Reasoning

Standard 4: Mathematical Connections

Standard 5: Algebra

Standard 10: Statistics

Teaching Notes

There are no hard and fast answers for this worksheet. Rather there are many different ones, some more comfortable or agreeable for employees than others. The only requirement is that the student respects the employees' requests and puts them into the proper chart format. This exercise can engender a discussion of how more than one answer can be correct. It can also be used in combination with Activity 22, Reading Work Schedules.

Context

Creating schedules and putting them into a schematic that can be read easily is a difficult job and one that is repeated by thousands of managers daily. Although this sheet is set in a bakery/restaurant, most hourly jobs are scheduled in a similar way.

Extension Activities

If your students work, you might ask them to bring in copies of the schedules used in their workplace. If their employer is willing, you might let your class try to schedule shifts.

Answers

A possible solution to this problem is:

EMPLOYEE	MON.	TUES.	WED.	THURS.	FRI.	SAT.	SUN.
LISA D-B	12–8	x	12–8	12–8	12–8	12–5	x
DAVID D-B	x	6:30–1:30	7–1	x	6:30–1:30	6:30–1	6:30–1
VINCE P.	7–1	7–1	x	x	12–7	x	x
CHRIS	6:30–1:30	x	6:30–1:30	x	7–12	x	x
CORINNA	12–7	12–7	12–7	12–7	12–7	x	x
TOM	x	12–8	x	7–9/12–1	x	12–4	12–4
BILLY	7–9/12–1	x	7–9/12–1	6:30–1:30	x	7–1	x
PETER	x	7–9/12–1	x	x	7–9/12–1	x	7–1
ANDY	x	x	x	7–1	x	x	12–5

Name _____ Date _____

26. Making Work Schedules

Andy runs a bakery/restaurant in Chicago. Each week he schedules his "front staff." Because he hires a number of part-time workers, many of whom are students, the schedule changes weekly. Each week Andy asks his employees if they have any special schedule requests. Then every Friday morning, he posts the schedule for the following Monday through Sunday. Below are next week's considerations and requests, and a blank schedule. Can you make a workable schedule for Andy's staff?

Andy has the following considerations:

- The store must be open from 7:00 A.M. to 7:00 P.M. each weekday, and from 7:00 A.M. to 4:00 P.M. on weekends.

- A manager must arrive at the store a half hour before opening, and a manager must stay an hour past closing to cash out and clean up.

- On weekdays, three workers are needed from 7:00 A.M. to 9:00 A.M., and five from 12:00 noon to 1:00 P.M. Four are needed from noon to 1:00 P.M. on weekend days.

- At least two workers must be working at any given time that the store is open.

- Tom, Peter, Andy, and Billy are the office staff and can work in the store for an hour or two if needed, but none of the other employees will be asked to come in for less than a four-hour shift. For instance, these four might work out front from 7:00 A.M. to 9:00 A.M. and then from 12:00 P.M. to 1:00 P.M., but not in between.

- No one can work more than 40 hours or five different days in a week.

- An employee who works until closing time one day should not have to come to work before 10:00 A.M. the next day.

- Lisa, Corinna, Andy, and Tom have been trained to be closing managers.

- David, Chris, Billy, Peter, and Andy have been trained to be opening managers.

- Lisa, David, Vince, Chris, and Corinna should have hours before Tom, Billy, Peter, and Andy are taken from their other duties to work out front.

- Chris has a class on Tuesday and Thursday mornings, and doesn't want to work before noon those days. He is also going away for the weekend, and will be leaving at 4:00 P.M. Friday.

- Tom prefers to work Tuesday nights if he has to be a closing manager.

(continued)

26. **Making Work Schedules** (continued)

- Corinna doesn't like to work weekends.

- David can't work Monday before noon. He also has an interview on Thursday morning.

- Vince has asked that he not work more than three days a week or for less than six hours a shift.

EMPLOYEE	MON.	TUES.	WED.	THURS.	FRI.	SAT.	SUN.
LISA D-B							
DAVID D-B							
VINCE P.							
CHRIS							
CORINNA							
TOM							
BILLY							
PETER							
ANDY							

27. Creating PERT Charts

Goal

To learn about PERT charts as a method for optimizing time use on project sites.

NCTM Standards Addressed

Standard 2: Mathematics as Communication

Standard 4: Mathematical Connections

Standard 5: Algebra

Standard 6: Functions

Standard 10: Statistics

Standard 12: Discrete Mathematics

Teaching Notes

Activity 24, Reading PERT charts, provides an introduction to these charts. Building a PERT chart is a matter of getting prerequisites in order. A PERT chart builds to the right, so each job that is dependent on previous jobs is to the right of those jobs. Redundant prerequisites are eliminated (task 6 is dependent on tasks 3 and 4, but task 4 is already dependent on task 3, so it is "redundant" to say that task 6 depends on task 3). The critical path is found by working back through the path of prerequisites from the end via the longest time path. Any tasks on this path are part of the "critical path." The length of the critical path is the time that should be allotted for the job.

Context

Because building the Polaris submarine was such a big job, engineers developed a PERT chart technique to facilitate the completion of their tasks. That chart was 100 yards long! The strategy, however, is useful for smaller projects.

Extension Activities

Students could consider another project, such as the completion of a mural on a school wall, and create a prerequisite list and PERT chart for the job.

Answers

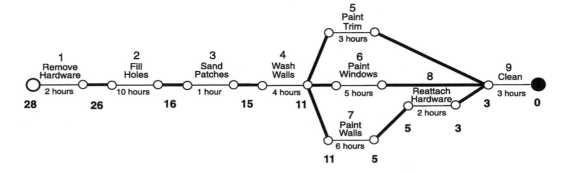

Critical path is tasks 1, 2, 3, 4, 7, 8, 9, taking 28 hours.

27. Creating PERT Charts

Jeff Collins is a painter. He takes jobs during the summer and is always diligent about following a program to completion of the job. Jeff uses PERT charts to make sure that he and his crew are working on the tasks in a progression that will let them finish the job in the time allotted.

The table below is a list of tasks that Jeff has identified for painting a room. Draw a PERT chart of the job and identify the critical path and projected completion time.

Task	Prerequisites	Hours to Complete Task
1. Remove Hardware	————	2
2. Fill Holes	1	10
3. Sand Patches	2	1
4. Wash Walls	1, 2, 3	4
5. Paint Trim	3, 4	3
6. Paint Windows	3, 4	5
7. Paint Walls	3, 4	6
8. Reattach Hardware	7	2
9. Clean	1, 2, 3, 4, 5, 6, 7, 8	3

1
Remove
Hardware

2 hours

9

Clean

3 hours

3   **0**

28. Logic Puzzles

Goal

To practice the use of charts in solving a logic puzzle.

NCTM Standards Addressed

Standard 1: Mathematics as Problem Solving

Standard 2: Mathematics as Communication

Standard 3: Mathematics as Reasoning

Standard 4: Mathematical Connections

Standard 5: Algebra

Standard 10: Statistics

Teaching Notes

Whole books of logic puzzles like this one are easy to find. Teach the students to set up a contradiction chart like the one on the following page and then let them work in pairs or groups to see it through.

Context

Although these problems do not arise in business, sports, or nutrition, they are valu-able for the reasoning and process they follow. Logic problems appear regularly in *GAMES Magazine,* and in many books.

Extension Activities

Find other problems like this and have students practice solving them. Also, for a real challenge, have students make a logic problem with only one correct answer.

Answers

Allison Talbot is from New York and has three pets.

Touch Khin is from California and has two pets.

Nondini Naqui is from Maine and has two pets.

Erica Burns is from Oregon and has one pet.

Elizabeth Borduas is from Florida and has one pet.

28. Logic Puzzles

Using the contradiction chart below, solve the following logic puzzle.

Recently, five students attended a national conference on pet ownership. They each had one, two, or three pets. They came from five different states: California, Florida, Maine, New York, and Oregon. Their first names were Allison, Elizabeth, Erica, Nondini, and Touch. Their last names were Borduas, Burns, Khin, Naqui, and Talbot. Given the following seven clues, can you determine the full names of each student, how many pets each has, and their home state?

1. Erica and Borduas have the same number of pets, but not the same number as Naqui.

2. No one else has the same number of pets as Allison.

3. Talbot (who comes from the East Coast), has more pets than Khin (who comes from the West Coast).

4. Elizabeth has as many pets as the person from Oregon.

5. No more than two people have the same number of pets, and no two people from the same coast have the same number of pets.

6. Nondini and Khin (who isn't Erica) have the same number of pets, which is more than the student from Florida has.

7. The students from Maine and California have the same number of pets.

	LAST NAMES					STATES					NO. OF PETS		
	Borduas	Burns	Khin	Naqui	Talbot	California	Florida	Maine	New York	Oregon	1	2	3
Allison													
Elizabeth													
Erica													
Nondini													
Touch													
1													
2													
3													
California													
Florida													
Maine													
New York													
Oregon													

FIRST NAMES

NO. OF PETS